Collins

English

AQA GCSE Revision

English

Poetry Anthology & Relationships

AQA GCSE

Poetry Revision Guide

Rachel Grant

Anthology ⟩ Contents

	Revise	Practise	Review

Cluster Overview

	Revise	Practise	Review
Overview of Poetry Anthology Cluster: Love and Relationships	p. 4 ☐		

Poem Overviews 1

	Revise	Practise	Review
When We Two Parted, Lord Byron	p. 8 ☐	p. 18 ☐	p. 34 ☐
Love's Philosophy, Percy Bysshe Shelley	p. 10 ☐	p. 19 ☐	p. 35 ☐
Porphyria's Lover, Robert Browning	p. 12 ☐	p. 20 ☐	p. 36 ☐
Sonnet 29 – 'I think of thee!', Elizabeth Barrett Browning	p. 15 ☐	p. 21 ☐	p. 37 ☐

Poem Overviews 2

	Revise	Practise	Review
Neutral Tones, Thomas Hardy	p. 22 ☐	p. 30 ☐	p. 50 ☐
The Farmer's Bride, Charlotte Mew	p. 24 ☐	p. 31 ☐	p. 51 ☐
Walking Away, Cecil Day Lewis	p. 26 ☐	p. 32 ☐	p. 52 ☐
Letters from Yorkshire, Maura Dooley	p. 28 ☐	p. 33 ☐	p. 53 ☐

Poem Overviews 3

	Revise	Practise	Review
Eden Rock, Charles Causley	p. 38 ☐	p. 46 ☐	p. 65 ☐
Follower, Seamus Heaney	p. 40 ☐	p. 47 ☐	p. 66 ☐
Mother, any distance, Simon Armitage	p. 42 ☐	p. 48 ☐	p. 67 ☐
Before You Were Mine, Carol Ann Duffy	p. 44 ☐	p. 49 ☐	p. 68 ☐

Contents

	Revise	Practise	Review

Poem Overviews 4

	Revise		Practise		Review	
Winter Swans, Owen Sheers	p. 54	☐	p. 62	☐	p. 69	☐
Singh Song!, Daljit Nagra	p. 56	☐	p. 63	☐	p. 70	☐
Climbing My Grandfather, Andrew Waterhouse	p. 59	☐	p. 64	☐	p. 71	☐

Poem Analysis

Comparing Poems	p. 72	☐
Sample Worked Question and Answer	p. 76	☐
Mixed Exam-Style Questions	p. 78	
Answers	p. 86	
Glossary	p. 95	
Index	p. 96	

Cluster Overview: Love and Relationships

Overview of Poetry Anthology Cluster: Love and Relationships

- The poems in the 'Love and Relationships' cluster focus on the various aspects of love and relationships between people.
- Marriage and romantic love, and the social and **cultural** pressures that impact on love, are the focus of some poems, whilst others consider the strong bonds between parent and child.
- Some of the poems consider how relationships change over time, or how a relationship – or even one moment that crystallised an aspect of a relationship – can change our **perceptions** of ourselves and others for ever.
- The pain of love, possessive love and love as 'letting go' are also depicted, as are the themes of separation and desire in relationships.
- Certain poems highlight unconventional love, or look at how reconciliation may be possible when a relationship is failing.

> **Key Point**
>
> The poems in the 'Love and Relationships' cluster focus on different types of love and relationships between people.

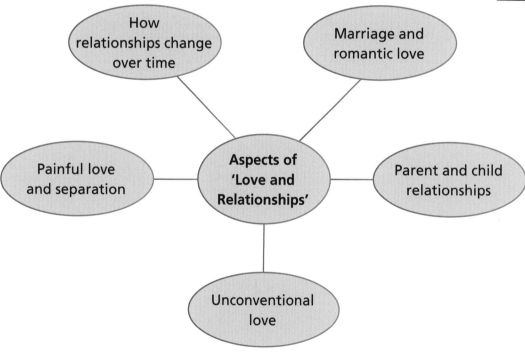

How relationships change over time

Marriage and romantic love

Painful love and separation

Aspects of 'Love and Relationships'

Parent and child relationships

Unconventional love

Approaching Older Poetry

- Some of the poems, such as *Sonnet 29* by Barrett Browning, *When We Two Parted* by Byron, *Love's Philosophy* by Shelley and *Porphyria's Lover* by Browning, were written in the 19th century. They may present attitudes towards love which seem very different to the way people think about relationships today. Other examples are *Neutral Tones* by Hardy and *The Farmer's Bride* by Mew.
- Older poems also deal with ideas and concepts that are universal, and that speak to us across the years.
  - In *Love's Philosophy*, Shelley is trying to persuade a woman to be his lover;
  - In *Sonnet 29* the speaker thinks of ways she can be close to her lover, even when they are apart.

Relationships Flavoured by an Era

- Some poems in the cluster are from the 20th century and carry strong images of a particular time in evoking a relationship. In *Before You Were Mine*, Duffy captures the glamour of the late 1940s to the early 1950s, whilst *Eden Rock* provides a sharply detailed picture of life between World War 1 and World War 2.

A Focus on Complexities and Difficulties

- Several of the poems focus on the complexities of parent–child and family relationships.
  - In *Mother, any distance*, Armitage talks about his relationship with his mother, as does Duffy in her poem *Before You Were Mine*.
  - In *Climbing My Grandfather*, Waterhouse explores the relationship between a young child and his grandfather.
  - In *Follower*, Heaney considers his feelings for his father as a young child and then later as an adult.
  - In *Walking Away*, Day Lewis starts with a remembered moment with his young son and develops his thoughts on what parental love means.

Cluster Overview: Love and Relationships

Effects of Voice, Mood, Technique and Form

- The poems in the 'Love and Relationships' cluster encompass a great range of voices, moods, techniques and forms.
    - *Singh Song!* by Nagra and *Porphyria's Lover* by Browning are both dramatic monologues, in which the poet employs a persona to speak to the listener. The speakers' voices have very different tones. Nagra's is playful and humorous, while Browning's is somewhat cold and impersonal, almost forensic.
    - Some of the poets use traditional poetic forms, for example a sonnet in *Sonnet 29* by Barrett Browning, which enhances the theme of romantic love, and a disrupted 'sonnet' in Armitage's *Mother, any distance*, which has the effect of adding to the poem's theme of independence and freedom.
    - Some poems, particularly those written in the 19th century such as *Love's Philosophy* by Shelley, or *Sonnet 29* by Barrett Browning, contain very ornate and flowery imagery, while others, such as *Letters From Yorkshire* by Dooley, use plainer, everyday language.
    - While some poems are poignant (*Eden Rock*), bitter (*Neutral Tones*) or sombre (*Winter Swans*) in mood, others, for example *Singh Song!* and *Love's Philosophy*, are exuberant and joyful adding to the persuasive power of the poets' arguments.
- Pay close attention to the structure, language and form the poets use in their poems to add effect and meaning.

Utilising the Various Poems, Ideas and Themes

- In the exam you will need to make connections between poems, looking at similarities and differences in the content and how poets present their ideas about love and relationships.
- The following table is a short guide to the themes presented in the poems. It may be used as a starting point, but it is not exhaustive.
- All the poems in the cluster are multi-layered and are open to many interpretations that highlight different aspects of several themes. They should be read and considered as such.

Key Point

All the poems in the 'Love and Relationships' cluster can be interpreted in different ways.

Key Words

Voice
Mood
Form
Dramatic monologue
Persona
Sonnet

Poem	Aspect(s) of Theme Presented	Additional Comments including Method and Form
When We Two Parted	– Love and loss – Bitterness	– Formal structure, rhythm and rhyme
Love's Philosophy	– Desire – Persuasive lover	– Use of pathetic fallacy – Romantic view of nature
Porphyria's Lover	– Desire and possession – Destructive love	– Dramatic monologue
Sonnet 29 – 'I think of thee!'	– Passion and desire	– Traditional sonnet – Love poem
Neutral Tones	– Love and loss – Bitterness	– Nature corresponds to human feelings – Formal structure
The Farmer's Bride	– Marriage – Destructive love	– First person monologue – Natural imagery counterpoints society's boundaries
Walking Away	– Love as 'letting go' – Parent and child relationship	– Formal structure – Use of natural imagery
Letters From Yorkshire	– Long-distance relationship	– Use of contrast – Free verse
Eden Rock	– Autobiographical – Child and parents	– Present tense immediacy – Significant details
Follower	– Parent and child relationship	– Precise rhythm and rhyme showing expertise
Mother, any distance	– Love as 'letting go' – Parent and child relationship	– Type of 'sonnet' going into free verse
Before You Were Mine	– Possessive love – Parent and child relationship	– Sensory details – Use of time frames
Winter Swans	– Reconciliation – Power of nature in relationships	– Central image/experience creates a 'before' and 'after'
Singh Song!	– Marriage – Love as freedom	– Dramatic monologue – Playful use of language
Climbing My Grandfather	– Families – Strength of love across generations	– Free verse – Extended metaphor

Poem Overviews 1: When We Two Parted

When We Two Parted

When we two parted
In silence and tears,
Half broken-hearted
To sever for years,
5   Pale grew thy cheek and cold,
Colder thy kiss;
Truly that hour foretold
Sorrow to this.

The dew of the morning
10 Sank chill on my brow–
It felt like the warning
Of what I feel now.
Thy vows are all broken,
And light is thy fame;
15 I hear thy name spoken,
And share in its shame.

They name thee before me,
A knell in mine ear;
A shudder come o'er me–
20 Why wert thou so dear?
They know not I knew thee,
Who knew thee too well–
Long, long shall I rue thee,
Too deeply to tell.

25 In secret we met–
In silence I grieve,
That thy heart could forget,
Thy spirit deceive.
If I should meet thee
30 After long years,
How should I greet thee?–
With silence and tears.

This tells us the affair happened years ago.

We can guess here that the other person grew 'cold' and withdrew from the affair.

The poet still (now) feels sad that the affair ended.

The poet links the feelings he had then (shown by the past tense) to his feelings now.

There is a mystery here: we are not being told the whole story. What is the 'shame' of the other person and why does the poet 'share' it?

Who is 'they'? Someone else is in the poem, but it is not clear who the person (or people) is.

'Knell' is the sound a church bell makes, especially for a funeral. The poet likens the name of the other person to a funeral bell. It is almost as if the person has died.

'They' is repeated from line 17.

People often 'shudder' when they feel a strong emotion.

Now we know the affair was a secret.

'rue' means regret.

Byron's feelings here are sadness a) that the other person could forget about him and b) that he was taken in by the other person, who betrayed his trust. Nothing here is explicit. We need to piece together what happened from the clues.

The repetition of this phrase from line 2 brings the poem full circle and implies that nothing will ever change about the relationship. It is now in the same state as it was when it ended and is a source of continuing pain.

Key: Assonance   Repetition of key words   Monosyllables

About the Poem

- The poem was written by Lord Byron and published in 1816. The poem is about a relationship that has ended.
- It is thought that the speaker is Byron and that the 'other' person in the poem was Lady Frances Webster, a married woman with whom Byron had a flirtation.
- Though the flirtation had been over for a year or two, the poem shows that Byron was still feeling hurt.

Ideas, Themes and Issues

- **Loss:** The first two verses describe the poet's feelings of loss following the end of an affair.
  - The phrases 'silence and tears' (2) and 'Half broken-hearted' (3) show his sadness at losing this person, and 'cold', 'Colder' and 'chill' show that the other person's feelings towards him have cooled.
  - The third verse tells us that the two people were very close 'knew thee too well' (22) and 'knell' (18) shows that the poet feels almost as if the other person has died, so strong is his sense of loss.
- **Bitterness:** As the poem develops, the poet shows increasing bitterness towards the other person.
  - He remembers that she forgot and deceived him. He also feels aggrieved that she still has the power to make him feel sad and ashamed, and that he can never tell anyone about the affair.
  - The lines (27–28) 'That thy heart could forget/ Thy spirit deceive' are perhaps the bitterest of all. This is not a poem about her – it's a poem about her continuing impact on him.
- **Secrecy:** In the same way as the affair was conducted in secret, it ended without anyone knowing, and must remain secret, so the poem keeps secrets from the reader.
  - We do not know who the person is or what kept them apart ('sever for years' (4)); why the affair ended or why they were only 'half' broken-hearted (was only one of them broken-hearted; and the other person not?); why the other person has 'shame' or why the poet shares it. The affair was a secret and the poem keeps its secrets, whilst giving the poet an opportunity to express his feelings.
  - The poem yields more questions than answers. We can only imagine what happened – we are not told directly.

Form, Structure and Language

- Almost every line in the poem has two **stressed syllables**, which, along with the pronounced use of **monosyllables**, give a driving, relentless rhythm and force to the poem.
- The stressed syllables often fall on words that build a picture of the poet's feelings towards his love (silence, tears, half, heart).
- The regular **rhyme** scheme and heavy use of **repetition** (of words and sounds) give a very formal and accomplished tone to the speaker's voice. He uses this structural formality to mask his pain and bitterness.

Key Words

Stressed syllables
Monosyllables
Rhyme
Repetition

Quick Test

1. When did the affair take place?
2. Was the affair publicly known about?
3. Who ended the affair – the poet or the other person?

Fountains here refers to natural springs of water.

Philosophy is the practice of seeking knowledge about reality. Shelley's title applies the term to love.

Love's Philosophy
The fountains mingle with the river
And the rivers with the ocean,
The winds of heaven mix for ever
With a sweet emotion;
5 Nothing in the world is single,
All things by a law divine
In another's being mingle.–
Why not I with thine?

See the mountains kiss high heaven,
10 And the waves clasp one another;
No sister-flower would be forgiven
If it disdained its brother:
And the sunlight clasps the earth,
And the moonbeams kiss the sea–
15 What is all this sweet work worth,
If thou kiss not me?

The speaker starts the argument with a list of examples of things in nature that are connected to each other.

The speaker is saying there is a heavenly law that says everything in nature should be connected.

Each verse ends with a rhetorical question that is the culmination of the speaker's persuasive argument to the lover, in the lines leading up to it.

Repetition of 'clasp' and 'kiss' make this verse more passionate than the first verse and lead up to the very bold and passionate question in the final line.

Disdain means to look down upon with contempt or scorn.

The speaker cleverly changes the order of the pronouns in this question, compared to the first verse. 'I' and 'thine' (8) have become 'thou' and 'me'.

Similar to the first verse, the speaker gives examples of connected, loving things in nature.

Repetition of 'and' lends force to his argument as it reaches a climax.

Key: Rhetorical questions   Repeated words   Repeated phrases

About the Poem

- The poem was written by Percy Bysshe Shelley and published in 1820.
- Shelley was a Romantic poet. The movement Romanticism favoured passion above logic and emotions above rationality.
- Romantic poetry draws inspiration from nature and is highly responsive to emotion and feeling.
- The speaker is a persuasive lover, who may be male or female.

Ideas, Themes and Issues

- **The natural world:** The speaker lists things in the natural world that are connected (river, ocean, winds, mountains, waves, flowers) to create an argument for the lovers to 'mingle' (1). Even the planets get involved: the sun and moon shine down and 'kiss' and 'clasp' the Earth.
- **Love:** This is a declaration of love presented as an argument.
  - The speaker uses **personification** presenting them as if they are lovers: 'mingle', 'mix', 'kiss' and 'clasp'.
  - Everything is in pairs and in a romantic embrace, and all are connected, for example fountains and rivers, rivers and ocean embrace each other.
  - Everything the speaker sees in nature reflects their feelings of love. This is an extended example of the **pathetic fallacy**, the poetic practice of attributing human emotion to aspects of nature. This was much favoured by Romantic poets.
- **Persuasion:** The speaker is very confident and uses **imperatives** and grand declarations to build a persuasive argument to the lover. The poet seems to be saying, 'Everything I see shows its love for everything else. We humans should love each other also.' This is the poet's philosophy.

Form, Structure and Language

- The use of **monosyllables** in lines 8 and 16 add force and directness to the persuasive impact of the **rhetorical questions**. **Repetition** of words and phrases reinforces the poet's urgency.
- The rhetorical questions at the end of each verse are given further emphasis by the poet's use of punctuation. There is a dash in the first verse and a colon in the second verse before the questions, which have the effect of momentarily stopping the speaker in full flow, as if drawing a breath.
- The poet uses personification, rhetorical questions and repetition of the word 'and' to add force to his persuasive argument.
- Five monosyllables in the last line of the first verse, and 12 monosyllables in the final two lines of the second verse, add emphasis to the sound of the lines, as the poet builds, then concludes, his argument.

> **Key Words**
>
> Personification
> Pathetic fallacy
> Imperative
> Monosyllable
> Rhetorical question
> Repetition

> **Quick Test**
>
> 1. How does the speaker build his argument?
> 2. What is his purpose in writing the poem?
> 3. How does he end each verse?

The first four lines set the scene: what is described happened earlier this evening and the speaker is looking back.

The phrase 'with heart fit to break' tells us about the speaker's state of mind, but we are not sure of the reason.

He ignores her when she arrives.

The colours he uses to describe her make her sound like a china doll: white and smooth skin, yellow hair, blue eyes.

Porphyria's Lover

The rain set early in tonight,
   The sullen wind was soon awake,
It tore the elm-tops down for spite,
   and did its worst to vex the lake:
5   I listened with heart fit to break.
When glided in Porphyria; straight
   She shut the cold out and the storm,
And kneeled and made the cheerless grate
   Blaze up, and all the cottage warm;
10   Which done, she rose, and from her form
Withdrew the dripping cloak and shawl,
   And laid her soiled gloves by, untied
Her hat and let the damp hair fall,
   And, last, she sat down by my side
15   And called me. When no voice replied,
She put my arm about her waist,
   And made her smooth white shoulder bare,
And all her yellow hair displaced,
   And, stooping, made my cheek lie there,
20   And spread o'er all her yellow hair,
Murmuring how she loved me — she
   Too weak, for all her heart's endeavour,
To set its struggling passion free
   From pride, and vainer ties dissever,
25   And give herself to me for ever.
But passion sometimes would prevail,
   Nor could tonight's gay feast restrain
A sudden thought of one so pale
   For love of her, and all in vain:
30   So, she was come through wind and rain.
Be sure I looked up at her eyes
   Happy and proud; at last I knew
Porphyria worshipped me; surprise
   Made my heart swell, and still it grew
35   While I debated what to do.
That moment she was mine, mine, fair,
   Perfectly pure and good: I found
A thing to do, and all her hair
   In one long yellow string I wound

Verbs used to describe Porphyria's movements and voice are muted and quiet, but in the first part of the poem she seems to be in control, taking charge of the fire.

Porphyria brings brightness, warmth and passion to the room.

Here Porphyria is taking the lead, but later the lover takes charge.

He sees her as weak.

'dissever' means to break away.

He sees love in terms of power – passivity vs. control. Seeing her giving herself to him makes him assume power and take the next step.`

He kills her at the moment when, for him, she has attained perfection.

The horror of this is intensified as it is linked linguistically to lines 20–21, which are tender and loving.

He repeats this as if to reassure himself.

In death she is as perfect to him as she was in life – he has captured her in that perfect moment for ever.

He recreates the intimate moment they have just shared when she was alive.

To his distorted thinking, he has given her what she truly wanted, i.e. to be permanently with her lover.

This reference to God, with the exclamation mark, seems to have a gleeful tone, as if the murderer is flaunting the fact that he has got away with it.

He's frightened that she might still be alive.

This extends the idea of Porphyria as a human doll, with eyes that open and shut.

He describes her as a collection of body parts: waist, shoulder, hair, eyes, cheek. He is objectifying her rather than seeing her as a person in her own right.

Her head is likened to a flower, continuing the natural, but passive, imagery used for Porphyria. Now, he has made her into the ultimate passive object: a corpse.

> 40 Three times her little throat around,
>   And strangled her. No pain felt she;
>   I am quite sure she felt no pain.
>   As a shut bud that holds a bee,
>   I warily oped her lids: again
> 45 Laughed the blue eyes without a stain.
>   And I untightened next the tress
>   About her neck; her cheek once more
>   Blushed bright beneath my burning kiss:
>   I propped her head up as before,
> 50 Only, this time my shoulder bore
>   Her head, which droops upon it still:
>   The smiling rosy little head,
>   So glad it has its utmost will,
>   That all it scorned at once is fled,
> 55 And I, its love, am gained instead!
>   Porphyria's love: she guessed not how
>   Her darling one wish would be heard.
>   And thus we sit together now,
>   And all night long we have not stirred,
> 60 And yet God has not said a word!

Key: | Simile | Repetition | Enjambment | Personification

About the Poem

- The poem was written by Robert Browning and published in 1836.
- Porphyria is the name given to a rare blood disorder that may cause mental, nervous or skin problems.
- The 'lover' in the title of this poem is the same as the person who 'speaks' it. He is an extremely abnormal person who recounts, in a very matter-of-fact way, how he has murdered Porphyria. He arranges her corpse to sit against him, as if sitting together as lovers.

Ideas, Themes and Issues

- **Sin:** The poem is disturbing because the speaker is so matter-of-fact and reasonable in his recount of what has happened.
  - Porphyria has come through the wind and rain to be with him and makes herself sexually available (for women to do this was very much taboo in Victorian society).

- The speaker murders her, but he makes it sound like a straightforward and reasonable thing to do: the line 'While I debated what to do.' (35) emphasises the clarity of his thinking.
- The murderer's behaviour is not condemned or punished in the poem – it is left to the reader to deliver judgement.
- The speaker expresses no remorse or guilt. There is an ambivalent final line in which God is mentioned.

- **Power:** In the first half of the poem, Porphyria takes action by making a fire and creating warmth. Then, she takes his arm and places it around her waist, placing his cheek on her shoulder ('put', 'made', 'displaced').
  - Once she tells him that she loves him and he knows that she worships him, the speaker seizes the power. He feels his heart swell with power and he then takes control of her ('That moment she was mine, mine, fair' (36)).
- **Violence:** The speaker tells of the act of murder in such a calm and reasonable way, it makes the act even more chilling.
  - 'Lover' is used in the title, but the way that love manifests itself in him is through cold and calculated violence.
  - After they make love, he cold-bloodedly kills her with the hair that she earlier had spread over them both in an embrace.
  - For the speaker, sex, power, violence and death are intertwined in the most disturbing way.

Form, Structure and Language

- The poem is a **dramatic monologue**, so we only get the perspective of the speaker.
- A regular **rhyme** scheme shows how the speaker adopts a logical, orderly emotional state, to mask his state of mind.
- The poem has a regular **rhythm** with four stressed syllables in each line. This is occasionally disrupted at key moments in the poem to draw the reader's attention.
- **Enjambment** suggests the fragmented thought processes of the speaker.

Quick Test

1. What is the weather like at the start of the poem?
2. How does the speaker say he killed Porphyria?
3. Porphyria is a girl's name. What is another meaning of the word?

Key Words

Dramatic monologue
Rhyme
Rhythm
Enjambment

The poem opens with an exclamation, indicating the speaker's excitement. It immediately identifies the 'I' is addressing another person – 'thee'.

Why are the vines 'wild'? To indicate the passion of her love, perhaps?

She wants her lover to come back (currently they are separated) and be near to him again.

Likens her thoughts to a vine that wraps around her lover.

Indicates a further stage in her thought process as she develops the image of vine and tree.

She realises her thoughts of her lover are not a good substitute for having her actual lover in person.

'insphere' means to encircle or surround.

Once he is back in her presence, she doesn't have to think about him, or encircle him with her thoughts, because he is there in person.

Sonnet 29 – 'I think of thee!'

I think of thee!—my thoughts do twine and bud

About thee, as wild vines, about a tree,

Put out broad leaves, and soon there's nought to see

Except the straggling green which hides the wood.

5 Yet, O my palm-tree, be it understood

I will not have my thoughts instead of thee

Who art dearer, better! Rather, instantly

Renew thy presence; as a strong tree should,

Rustle thy boughs and set thy trunk all bare,

10 And let these bands of greenery which insphere thee

Drop heavily down, —burst, shattered, everywhere!

Because, in this deep joy to see and hear thee

And breathe within thy shadow a new air,

I do not think of thee—I am too near thee.

Key:

| Metaphor | Repetition | Enjambment |

| Forceful verbs | Exclamations |

Poem Overviews 1:
Sonnet 29 – 'I think of thee!'

About the Poem

- The poem was written by Elizabeth Barrett Browning when she was being courted by Robert Browning.
- It is one of a sequence of 44 **sonnets** in the collection *Sonnets from the Portuguese*, published in 1850.
- The sonnets are love poems, inspired by her feelings for Browning.
- It is generally assumed that Barrett Browning is the speaker.

Ideas, Themes and Issues

- **Romantic love:** The poem is written in the **first person** and is therefore highly personal.
    - The poem starts with 'I think of thee!' and comes full circle at the end with a negative version of the same phrase 'I do not think of thee'.
    - The poem is a fierce, passionate and excited declaration of the speakers love ('this deep joy', (12)).
    - The poet sets up the central image of a palm-tree covered by a vine in the first two lines.
    - The poet compares the speaker's love to a vine that buds and grows 'broad leaves' (3). This is a feminine image compared to the 'strong' (8) wood of the tree – the image chosen for the male lover.
- **Confinement and freedom:** The speaker's thoughts progress through a logical process in the poem.
    - In the first **quatrain** the speaker compares their love to 'wild vines' (2) which cover the 'palm-tree' (5) (their lover) so completely, that its boughs are no longer visible. There's a suggestion that the vine (their love) suffocates the tree (their lover).
    - This idea is developed through the next quatrain, as the speaker realises they would rather have their lover in person, than only have thoughts of them. Therefore, the speaker urges their lover to break free of the vine, 'which insphere thee' (10) and to renew their presence – in other words, to show themselves again.
    - Line 11 contains violent verbs – 'drop heavily', 'burst' and 'shattered', as the tree breaks the vine that surrounds it and is set free.

- Having developed the **extended metaphor** through the first 11 lines, it is then dropped in the final three lines of the poem with the word 'Because'. Here, the speaker appears to collect themselves with the realisation that being in their lover's presence is freedom for them too. They can now 'breathe … a new air'(13) and do not need to think (or construct metaphors) about their love when they are close by.
- The poet's use of the image of confinement that is broken has been linked to Elizabeth's relationship with her father, who was very protective of her following a childhood accident. She was treated as an invalid by him and so her relationship with Robert Browning offered her liberation from this situation.

Form, Structure and Language

- A sonnet has 14 lines and follows a clear rhyme pattern. Sonnets are often love poems and contain a clear line of logical argument.
- The poet uses an extended metaphor – her love is compared to a vine on a palm-tree – that is sustained until line 11.
- The poem complies with the typical sonnet form of two quatrains (a group of four lines) and a **sestet** (a group of six lines).
- Significant **repetition** of the words 'thee' and 'thy' emphasise that the subject of the poem is her feelings for her lover.
- **Enjambment** is used to represent the ceaseless flow of love from speaker to lover and the way the vine wraps around the palm tree.

Quick Test

1. What is the form of this poem?
2. How many lines are in a quatrain?
3. Who is the speaker addressing in the poem?

Key Words

Sonnet
First person
Quatrain
Extended metaphor
Sestet
Repetition
Enjambment

When We Two Parted

1 What has happened to the poet? Tick the correct answer.

A He has been reminded of an old love affair. ☐

C He has heard his lover is dead. ☐

B His lover has left the country. ☐

D His former lover has married someone else. ☐

2 What two things did the other person do to offend the poet?

.... [2]

3 Find three examples of repeated words in the poem.

.... [3]

4 What rhyme scheme is used in the poem?

.... [1]

5 Complete the sentence: The poet uses repetition of the phrase 'silence and tears' to show ...

.... [2]

6 Find three words or phrases that convey cold, lack of life and lack of colour. What do these words suggest about the relationship?

....

.... [4]

7 How does the poet indicate 'then' and 'now'?

.... [1]

8 **a)** Which syllables in these lines are stressed? Underline them. [4]

Thy vows are all broken,
And light is thy fame;
I hear thy name spoken,
And share in its shame.

b) Why do you think the poet chose to stress these words?

.... [1]

9 Complete the sentence: As we learn more about the poet's feelings, the tone of the poem

changes from sadness to .... [1]

10 Identify one word that tells you how the poet feels when he hears the other person's name.

.... [1]

Love's Philosophy

1 Why do you think the poet ends each verse with a rhetorical question?

.... [1]

2 Name three natural things that the speaker mentions in the first verse.

.... [3]

3 Which two repeated verbs indicate a change of tone in the second verse?

.... [1]

4 How does the speaker widen the scope of the argument in the second verse?

.... [1]

5 What does the speaker mean by 'a law divine' (6)? How does it add to the argument?

....

.... [2]

6 What is the effect of the repeated 'And' at the start of lines 10, 13 and 14 in the second verse?

.... [1]

7 How does the poet's use of punctuation add impact to the speaker's argument?

....

....

.... [1]

8 Which of these best describes the speaker's tone? Circle the correct answer. [1]

tentative   **assertive**   **quiet**   **tense**   **doubtful**

9 What particular characteristics of Romantic poetry does this poem exhibit?

....

.... [2]

10 Does the speaker give a convincing argument to the object of his love, or not?
Give your reasons.

....

.... [2]

Porphyria's Lover

1 In what ways does the speaker set the mood or atmosphere at the start of the poem? How does this indicate his mental state?

....

.... [2]

2 What effect does Porphyria have on the atmosphere in the cottage?

.... [1]

3 How does Porphyria encourage her lover?

.... [1]

4 What does the line 'I listened with heart fit to break' (5) tell us about the speaker's state of mind?

....

.... [1]

5 At what point in the poem does the speaker decide to murder Porphyria?

.... [1]

6 Why do you think the speaker decides to murder her? Give two reasons.

.... [2]

7 How does the structure (rhythm and rhyme) of the poem contribute to our understanding of the speaker's mental state?

....

.... [2]

8 What two things does the speaker compare Porphyria to in his physical descriptions of her?

.... [2]

9 In what way does the speaker equate 'love' with 'possession'?

.... [1]

10 Why do you think the speaker chooses to mention God in the final line? Give two possible reasons.

.... [2]

Sonnet 29 – 'I think of thee!'

1 What image does the speaker introduce in the first two lines?

_____ [1]

2 What is suggested by the poet's use of the word 'twine' (1)?

_____ [1]

3 What type of tree does the speaker imagine her lover to be?

_____ [1]

4 Who is the 'vine' and who is the 'palm-tree' in the poem?

_____

_____ [2]

5 What is the name given to a sustained image like the one used in this poem?

_____ [1]

6 How does the final line contradict the first line?

_____

_____ [1]

7 What does the speaker mean by 'I am too near thee' (14)?

_____

_____ [1]

8 What does the word 'insphere' (10) mean?

_____ [1]

9 Why does the speaker feel she can breathe 'new air' (13)?

_____ [1]

10 In what ways does the poem conform to the sonnet poetic form?

_____

_____ [2]

Poem Overviews 2: Neutral Tones

'chidden' means told off or rebuked. The image is of God being so annoyed with the sun that he has stripped it of all its colour.

The earth itself lacks life and fertility in winter and seems to be 'starving'.

Smiles usually indicate happiness, but this one is dead. It turns into a grin that is so sour that Hardy likens it to a bird that appears when something bad is going to happen ('ominous').

The repetition of 'pond' from the first line brings the poem full circle, but with no forward movement.

Neutral Tones

We stood by a pond that winter day,
And the sun was white, as though chidden of God,
And a few leaves lay on the starving sod;
    – They had fallen from an ash, and were gray.

5 Your eyes on me were as eyes that rove
Over tedious riddles of years ago;
And some words played between us to and fro
    On which lost the more by our love.

The smile on your mouth was the deadest thing
10 Alive enough to have strength to die;
And a grin of bitterness swept thereby
    Like an ominous bird a-wing….

Since then, keen lessons that love deceives,
And wrings with wrong, have shaped to me
15 Your face, and the God-curst sun, and a tree,
    And a pond edged with grayish leaves.

'Neutral' describes both the winter scene, drained of bright colour, and the relationship, drained of hope and love. 'Tones' can refer to colour and to mood.

The relationship has been 'tedious' (dull, boring) for some time.

The speaker is remembering this moment by the pond as the end of a relationship. It happened some time ago, but the memory is still very painful.

'curst' means 'cursed' and echoes 'chidden' in line 2.

Key:
| Alliteration | Imagery | Oxymoron |

| Assonance | Repetition |

About the Poem

- The poem was written by Thomas Hardy in 1867, when he was 27 years old.
- It is a **lyric poem**, but is bitter in tone, about the ending of a love affair.
- The poem explores the poet's pain and despair as he remembers how a relationship in the past had been over for some time before it actually ended. The speaker is probably Hardy himself.

Ideas, Themes and Issues

- **Sterility and death:** The poem opens with a pond, trees and leaves and it ends in exactly the same place. However, where the start was 'we' (two people in a relationship), the ending is two people apart.
  - There are several images of sterility, such as the leaves, the earth, the sun and even the water in the poem (a pond, not a flowing river or stream). They all carry overtones of stagnancy.
  - Everything in the poem is drained of colour and life, and the natural surroundings mirror the sterility and bitterness of the relationship, which is also dead. The poet's ex-lover's smile is 'the deadest thing' (9).
- **Bitter disappointment:** The poet looks back on this scene which, over time, has come to represent bitter disappointment for him.
  - Although this happened some time ago, ('Since then' (13)) whenever he has been let down, or disappointed by love affairs, he has recalled this moment by the pond.
  - The feelings he had at this moment have crystallised into a recurring memory for him.

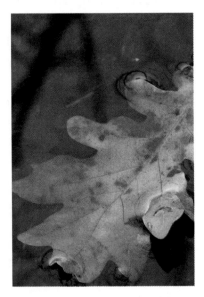

Form, Structure and Language

- **Antithesis** runs through the poem, both literal in the **oxymoron** 'Alive enough to have strength to die' (10) and implied (the sun should equal warmth and gold, but instead is 'white' (2) and 'God-curst' (15); the smile that should be happy is bitter and ominous).
- The poem uses highly patterned language with many echoes and repetitions.
- The **alliteration** in 'wrings with wrong' (14) and 'God-curst sun' (15) give a harsh sound, that makes the poet sound cold and almost sneering, but full of pain also.
- The way the poem comes full circle, repeating the pond, tree and leaves from the first verse brings it to a desolate close.

Key Words

Lyric poem
Antithesis
Oxymoron
Alliteration

Quick Test

1. What words would you use to describe the poet's mood in the poem?
2. How does the title reflect the content of the poem?
3. How does the structure of the poem reflect the poet's emotions?

Poem Overviews 2: The Farmer's Bride

About the Poem

- The poem was written by Charlotte Mew (1869–1928).
- The poem describes the relationship between a farmer and his young wife. They have been married for three years, but their relationship is distant and is probably unconsummated.
- The girl responds to marriage by first running away and then withdrawing from the human world.

Ideas, Themes and Issues

- **Desire:** The farmer's desire for his wife is clear in the final verse.
- **Marriage:** The marriage was not based on love or romance. The farmer seems to have chosen his wife on the basis of her age and looks. We assume that the wife had no say in the marriage.
- **Men and women:** There is a clear distinction between the sexes. While she is not close to the women, she sees them as less of a threat. The men bond together to catch her.
- **The natural world:** The poem is full of details from the natural world and the **voice** of the poem responds to the changes in the seasons. The farmer's descriptions of his wife compare her to a range of plants and animals. She finds solace and trust with animals.

The Farmer's Bride

Suggests selection and a marriage she was forced into, rather than one she desired.

A simile comparing her to the natural world.

Almost animalistic. Could suggest fear or innocence.

The men pursue her as they would an animal they were hunting.

Three Summers since I chose a maid,
Too young maybe – but more's to do
At harvest-time than bide and woo.
  When us was wed she turned afraid
5 Of love and me and all things human;
Like the shut of a winter's day
Her smile went out, and 'twasn't a woman –
  More like a little frightened fay.
  One night, in the Fall, she runned away.

10 'Out 'mong the sheep, her be,' they said,
Should properly have been abed;
But sure enough she wasn't there
Lying awake with her wide brown stare.
  So over seven-acre field and up-along across the down
15 We chased her, flying like a hare
Before our lanterns. To Church-Town
  All in a shiver and a scare
We caught her, fetched her home at last
  And turned the key upon her, fast.

20 She does the work about the house
As well as most, but like a mouse:
  Happy enough to chat and play

Key: | Simile | Rhetorical question | Caesura |

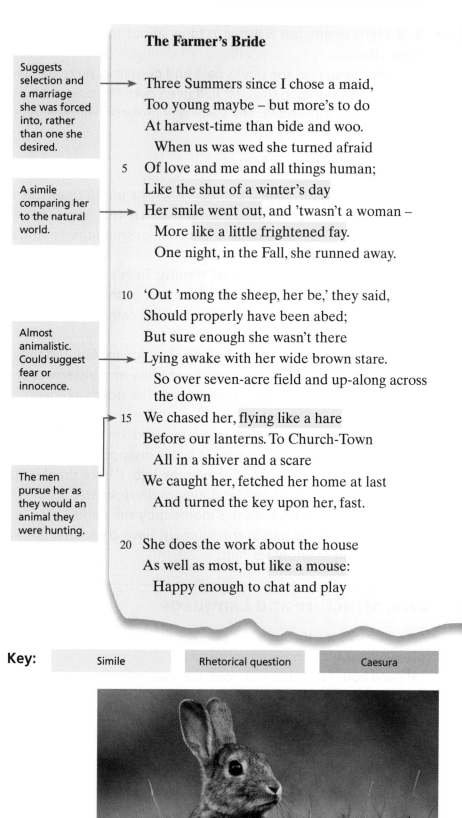

With birds and rabbits and such as they,
So long as men-folk keep away.
25 'Not near, not near!' her eyes beseech ←
When one of us comes within reach.
The women say that beasts in stall
Look round like children at her call. ←
I've hardly heard her speak at all.

A reaction to men in general, not just the farmer.

A simile comparing animals to innocent children may suggest she also shares this quality.

30 Shy as a leveret, swift as he,
Straight and slight as a young larch tree,
Sweet as the first wild violets, she,
To her wild self. But what to me?

Condensed list of similes makes his admiration clear.

The short days shorten and the oaks are brown,
35 The blue smoke rises to the low grey sky,
One leaf in the still air falls slowly down,
A magpie's spotted feathers lie
On the black earth spread white with rime,
The berries redden up to Christmas-time.
40 What's Christmas-time without there be
Some other in the house than we!

Slower pace suggests the farmer's ease with the natural world and contrasts with his feelings about his marriage.

She sleeps up in the attic there
Alone, poor maid. 'Tis but a stair
Betwixt us. Oh! my God! the down,
45 The soft young down of her, the brown,
The brown of her – her eyes, her hair, her hair!

Exclamation, repetition and internal rhyme suggest his torment/desire.

Internal rhyme   Sibilance and assonance   Repetition

Form, Structure and Language

- The poem is presented as a first-person **monologue**, which presents the farmer's understanding of his relationship with his wife.
- The wife is described through **similes** comparing her to animals, plants and a fairy. This distances her from the human world.
- Rhetorical questions show his confusion. He seems lonely and the marriage has not given him the children or companionship he wanted.
- The farmer describes the changing seasons; he understands the natural world better than he understands his wife.
- **Sibilance** and **assonance** slow the pace as the seasons change to winter.
- **Enjambment**, and an initial **caesura**, highlight her isolation and suggest the farmer's sympathy.
- **Repetition** and internal rhyme in the final verse suggest the farmer is tormented by his desire for his wife.
- Both the farmer and his bride understand the natural world, but this only makes their difficulties more poignant.

Key Words
Voice
Monologue
Similes
Sibilance
Assonance
Enjambment
Caesura

> **Quick Test**
>
> 1. Name three things that the wife is compared to through the use of similes.
> 2. What phrases link the wife to prey being hunted?
> 3. What is ironic about the wife being described in animal imagery?

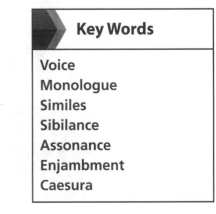

Sets the time of the memory at the start of autumn school term.

The freshly-painted white markings of a football pitch, but does it have another meaning also?

This simile is drawn from nature — perhaps referring to a sycamore seed, which is 'winged'.

This particular memory remains so vivid for the speaker – it is almost like a physical sensation.

Having an individual identity.

Walking Away

It is eighteen years ago, almost to the day —
A sunny day with leaves just turning,
The touch-lines new-ruled — since I watched you play
Your first game of football, then, like a satellite
5   Wrenched from its orbit, go drifting away

Behind a scatter of boys. I can see
You walking away from me towards the school
With the pathos of a half-fledged thing set free
Into a wilderness, the gait of one
10 Who finds no path where the path should be.

That hesitant figure, eddying away
Like a winged seed loosened from its parent stem,
Has something I never quite grasp to convey
About nature's give-and-take — the small, the scorching
15 Ordeals which fire one's irresolute clay.

I have had worse partings, but none that so
Gnaws at my mind still. Perhaps it is roughly
Saying what God alone could perfectly show —
How selfhood begins with a walking away,
20 And love is proved in the letting go.

Written about the past (a memory).

This simile is taken from space exploration (in its infancy in the 1950s, when the poem was written).

'pathos' means pitiful suffering. 'fledged' means able to fly.

Senses that his son feels lost and vulnerable.

'irresolute' means uncertain or undecided.

Christian religious references to God the father who 'so loved the world that he gave his Son'.

'proved' has several meanings: tested, made certain, shown to be true.

Knows he has to let his son be free to grow and mature, even though his instinct is to protect him.

Key: Repetition   Simile   Figurative language

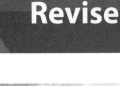

About the Poem

- The poem was written by Cecil Day Lewis and was published in 1962.
- The poet dedicated the poem to his son Sean, who was a schoolboy at the time of the memory recalled in the poem.

Ideas, Themes and Issues

- **Parental love:** The tone of the poem is sad and regretful, but also accepting as the speaker, a father, watches his son walk away from him – literally – towards school.
  - This image prompts the father to see how his son is growing up and away from him, as he must do in order to reach independence. The speaker reflects on how this is a painful process: 'scorching', (14), 'Ordeals' (15), but a necessary one.
  - The speaker's attitude at the end is one of acceptance: that 'love is proved in the letting go' (20).
- **Growing up:** The speaker describes the son as a 'hesitant figure' (11) who seems adrift and uncertain.
  - The speaker uses two **similes** – one likening his son to a satellite (4–5) and the other likening him to a 'winged seed' (12), to indicate the change in the relationship he perceives is happening, as his son is 'walking away' (19).
  - Parents have the urge to protect, but there is the acceptance that children must grow up and move away to achieve independence. Lines 14–15 contain the idea that to give, you must take and this is a natural, if painful, experience.
- **Separation: Repetition** of 'away' is used in the poem. The words 'Wrenched from' (5), 'set free' (8) and 'loosened from' (12) also refer to separation.
- He refers to 'worse partings' (16), but admits that this particular parting continues to affect him.

Form, Structure and Language

- The syntax of the poem mirrors the poet's struggle to put his feelings into words, with sentences interrupted by a new thought (14–15) and use of the words 'Perhaps' and 'roughly' (17).
- Only three of the lines are **end-stopped** (10, 15, 20). Most lines are run on, indicating the free flow of the speaker's thoughts and emotions.
- His language indicates that he feels pain and hardship ('wrenched', 'ordeals', 'scorching', 'gnaws') on his son's behalf.
- The poem powerfully evokes how a parent's role is fraught with worry and concern for their child.
- The similes in the first and third verses indicate the speaker's feeling of concern for his son's perceived vulnerability, as he starts to move towards independence from his parents.

> **Key Point**
>
> The poem is popular because it simply, and powerfully, evokes the strength of the love of a parent for a child.

> **Key Words**
>
> Simile
> Repetition
> End-stopped

> **Quick Test**
>
> 1. Who is the speaker of the poem?
> 2. What memory is he writing about?
> 3. Who is doing the 'walking away' (19)?

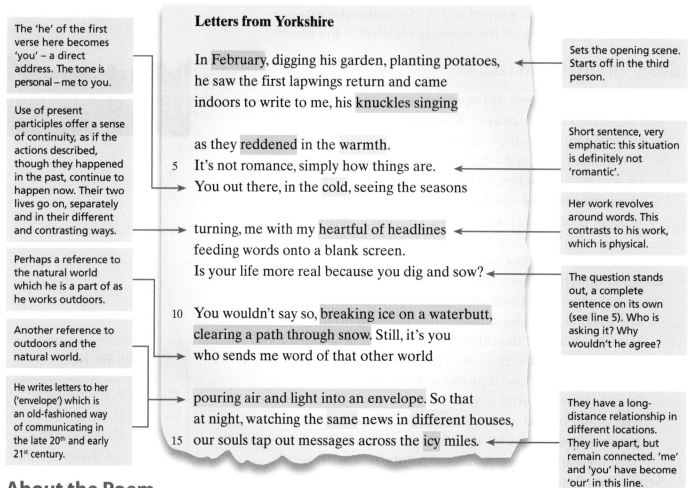

Letters from Yorkshire

In February, digging his garden, planting potatoes,

he saw the first lapwings return and came

indoors to write to me, his knuckles singing

as they reddened in the warmth.

5   It's not romance, simply how things are.

You out there, in the cold, seeing the seasons

turning, me with my heartful of headlines

feeding words onto a blank screen.

Is your life more real because you dig and sow?

10   You wouldn't say so, breaking ice on a waterbutt,

clearing a path through snow. Still, it's you

who sends me word of that other world

pouring air and light into an envelope. So that

at night, watching the same news in different houses,

15   our souls tap out messages across the icy miles.

Annotations (left side):

The 'he' of the first verse here becomes 'you' – a direct address. The tone is personal – me to you.

Use of present participles offer a sense of continuity, as if the actions described, though they happened in the past, continue to happen now. Their two lives go on, separately and in their different and contrasting ways.

Perhaps a reference to the natural world which he is a part of as he works outdoors.

Another reference to outdoors and the natural world.

He writes letters to her ('envelope') which is an old-fashioned way of communicating in the late 20th and early 21st century.

Annotations (right side):

Sets the opening scene. Starts off in the third person.

Short sentence, very emphatic: this situation is definitely not 'romantic'.

Her work revolves around words. This contrasts to his work, which is physical.

The question stands out, a complete sentence on its own (see line 5). Who is asking it? Why wouldn't he agree?

They have a long-distance relationship in different locations. They live apart, but remain connected. 'me' and 'you' have become 'our' in this line.

About the Poem

- The poem was written by Maura Dooley, who worked for some years in Yorkshire before moving to London.
- It was first published in a collection of poems called *Sound Barrier* in 2002.
- The poem **contrasts** two lifestyles – that of 'he'/'you' (which is outdoors and physical) and that of 'me' (which is indoors and involves writing words on a computer screen).

Key:

Contrast

Personification

Imagery

References to winter weather

Ideas, Themes and Issues

- **Long-distance relationships:** The speaker expresses their thoughts and feelings about a relationship, but it is not made clear what the relationship is.
    - The line 'It's not romance …' (5) indicates that this is not a love relationship. However, the two people in the poem are clearly very close and remain closely connected, even though they live separately and at a distance from each other.
    - In the final line, the use of the word 'souls' suggests that the two people are old friends who know each other very well.

- The speaker switches from **third person** in the first verse to the more personal 'you' in the second verse. In the final verse, it becomes the inclusive 'our' acknowledging that though separate, the two are emotionally close.
- **Contrasting lifestyles:** We learn that 'you'/'he' works outdoors and that he digs, sows and plants in Yorkshire in February, and that he writes letters to her.
  - The lifestyle of 'you'/'he' contrasts with the speaker's own lifestyle, which is indoors and involves writing at a computer. There is also mention of headlines, so we may think her job involves reporting the news, perhaps for a newspaper or TV.
  - The speaker enjoys hearing this 'news' (14) from Yorkshire, about lapwings returning and other news of the 'other world' (12) – his outdoor life in Yorkshire.
  - It seems the speaker misses Yorkshire. The speaker wonders if their life is less 'real' (9) than his because it is distanced from the outdoor world that he inhabits.
- **Letters and communication:** The 'Letters from Yorkshire' are literally letters, posted from a friend in Yorkshire, containing 'news'.
  - Further references to communication are in the words that the speaker types ('feeding words onto a blank screen', (8)) and the 'headlines' (7) that her heart is full of).
  - In the final verse, there is an image of their souls tapping out messages which brings to mind Morse code, or tapping on a keyboard.
  - These messages link the two, as they exchange them 'across the icy miles' (15). They are also linked by watching the 'same news' (14).

Form, Structure and Language

- Use of **enjambment** as the sentences run over lines, and verse breaks, serve to draw our attention to the single line sentence (5) and question (9).
- The use of **pronouns** in the poem indicates how the speaker's thoughts develop as they think about the relationship.
- The **comparison** made between the two lifestyles indicates that the speaker does not like their lifestyle as much as he likes his. Yet, in line 10, the speaker acknowledges that there is nothing romantic about his life either.
- The poet uses plain and simple words, often monosyllabic, to convey the nature of the relationship. The word choice underlines the thought behind the line, 'not romance, simply how things are' (5). There is nothing flowery about the poem, the language, or the relationship.

Key Point

Words are communication and each of the people in the poem uses them in different, but powerful, ways.

Key Words

Contrast
Third person
Enjambment
Pronouns
Comparison

Quick Test

1. What time of year is it?
2. What is the speaker's line of work?
3. What might 'he' do for a living?

Neutral Tones

1 How does the poet disrupt the rhythm of lines 3–4 and lines 15–16? What does this convey?

[2]

2 Which colours are mentioned in the poem?

[3]

3 What is the significance of the words 'Since then' (13)?

[1]

4 Why do you think the word 'And' is repeated at the start of several of the lines in the poem?

[1]

5 Complete the sentence.

The poet uses the images 'as though chidden of God' and '_____' [1]
to indicate that this situation is so bleak that even God is displeased.

6 Identify an example of an oxymoron in the poem.

[1]

7 Explain what you understand by the line 'On which lost the more by our love' (8).

[2]

8 Which of these words best describes the mood of the poem? Tick the correct answer.

A excited ☐   **C** desolate ☐

B passionate ☐   **D** ghostly ☐   [1]

9 Why does the poet choose to return to the same scene at the end of the poem
as at the start? Give TWO reasons.

[2]

The Farmer's Bride

1. Who is speaking in the poem? .... [1]

2. How long has he been married? .... [1]

3. What happened when his wife ran away?

   .... [1]

4. Why doesn't she run away any more?

   .... [1]

5. How do we know the wife is frightened of men?

   ....

   .... [1]

6. Do you think this marriage has been consummated? Explain your answer with reference to the poem.

   ....

   .... [2]

7. Comment on the poet's use of rhyming couplets in the poem. What do they add to the meaning?

   ....

   .... [2]

8. The poet makes considerable use of animal imagery in the poem. Give two reasons why you think they do this.

   ....

   .... [2]

9. Which line tells you that the farmer and his wife married young?

   .... [1]

10. Which words tell you that this marriage was probably arranged?

    .... [1]

Walking Away

1 What kind of love is evoked in this poem? Tick the correct answer.

   A brotherly love ☐   **C** marital love ☐

   B parental love ☐   **D** romantic love ☐   [1]

2 Identify two similes that the poet uses to indicate separation.

   ....

   .... [2]

3 How long ago did the incident recalled in the poem take place?

   .... [1]

4 Why is this parting so particularly painful for the speaker to remember?

   ....

   ....

   .... [2]

5 What is the effect of the repetition of the word 'away'?

   .... [1]

6 Explain what you think the speaker is trying to express in the final two lines of the poem.

   ....

   ....

   .... [2]

7 In line 13, what is the speaker struggling with?

   .... [1]

8 What do you think the verb 'proved' in the final line might mean in the context of the poem?

   ....

   .... [2]

Letters from Yorkshire

1. What do we learn about 'his' lifestyle in lines 1–2?

   [1]

2. Why does 'he' write to the speaker about the return of the lapwings?

   [1]

3. What do you think the speaker does for a living?

   [1]

4. Is there anything romantic about this relationship? Which words tell you this? If it isn't romantic, what sort of relationship do you think they have?

   [2]

5. In what ways do the pair communicate with each other?

   [1]

6. What does the word 'souls' in the final line suggest about the nature of their relationship?

   [1]

7. Give two examples of ways that the speaker suggests that his life in Yorkshire is not 'romantic'.

   [2]

8. The poem contrasts two 'worlds'. Briefly explain what the differences are between them.

   [2]

9. The poem contains several references to letters and words. What is the significance of these in the poem?

   [1]

10. What does the speaker suggest with the question, 'Is your life more real ...' (9)?

   [1]

When We Two Parted

1 Who is the poem about?

.... [1]

2 How does the poet feel about the relationship now? Tick the correct answer. [1]

A shocked ☐   C forgiving ☐

B resentful ☐   D relieved that it is over ☐

3 How many syllables are stressed in the majority of the lines in the poem?

.... [1]

4 How long is it since the lovers broke up?

.... [1]

5 a) Indicate how the poet brings the poem full circle.

.... [1]

b) Why do you think they chose to do this?

.... [1]

6 What do you think the following line means? 'And light is thy fame' (14)

....

.... [1]

7 Why does the poet feel he has to suffer in secret?

.... [1]

8 What do you think the poet means by the phrase 'Half broken-hearted' (3)?

....

.... [2]

9 By keeping the other person's identity a secret, who do you think the poet was trying to protect?

.... [1]

Love's Philosophy

1 Name three pairs of things in nature that the speaker mentions in the second verse.

_____ [3]

2 In what ways does the structure of the second verse repeat the structure of the first verse?

_____

_____ [2]

3 Which three verbs that mean 'connect or link' does the poet use in the first verse?

_____ [3]

4 How does the speaker choose to end each verse?

_____ [1]

5 What does the 'philosophy' of the title refer to?

_____ [1]

6 Which of these best describes the tone of the poem? Circle the correct answer. [1]

serious   **ironic**   **playful**   **bitter**   **bleak**

7 Why does the speaker want to present a 'logical' argument? What is unusual about the 'facts' he presents?

_____

_____ [2]

8 In the lines 'Why not I with thine?' (8) and 'If thou kiss not me?' (16) the poet changes the order of the pronouns. What is the effect of this?

_____ [1]

9 In what ways does the speaker use nature to present his argument?

_____ [1]

10 What literary technique, particularly favoured by Romantic poets, is used in this poem?

_____ [1]

Porphyria's Lover

1 How does Porphyria take control of the situation when she arrives at the cottage?

[2]

2 What is the effect of the repeated 'and' in the poem? What does it suggest about the speaker?

[2]

3 Comment on how the poet uses the structure of the poem to indicate something about the speaker's state of mind.

[1]

4 What does the use of enjambment suggest about the speaker's state of mind?

[1]

5 Where has Porphyria come from to visit the cottage?

[1]

6 'No pain felt she;/I am quite sure she felt no pain' (41–42). Why do you think this is important to the speaker?

[1]

7 Which two lines in the poem tell you that the speaker thinks love means possession?

[2]

8 What is the name given to this kind of poem, where the words are spoken by a character to a silent listener?

[1]

9 What justification does the speaker give for his action of murder?

[1]

10 How does the scene described at the end of the poem mirror and differ from the one when Porphyria arrives at the cottage?

[2]

Sonnet 29 – 'I think of thee!'

1 What is the significance of the words 'Yet' in line 5 and 'Because' in line 12?

.... [2]

2 Which of these best describes the love described in the poem? Tick the correct answer. [1]

A motherly love ☐   **C** sisterly love ☐

B romantic love ☐   **D** unrequited love ☐

3 What do the images of a) wild vines and b) palm trees represent in the poem?

....

.... [2]

4 Does the speaker change her point of view as the poem develops? Explain how.

....

....

....

.... [2]

5 What is the rhyme scheme of the poem? How does it help you divide the poem up?

....

.... [2]

6 What is a sestet? .... [1]

7 Why does the poem contain so many repetitions of the word 'thee'?

.... [1]

8 What does the speaker mean by the line 'I will not have my thoughts instead of thee' (6)?

.... [1]

9 Which two words tell you that the speaker feels very passionately about her lover?

.... [1]

10 Why does the speaker use exclamations to convey her feelings?

.... [1]

'somewhere beyond' gives a sense of mystery – we are not certain of the place.

Alerts us to the fact that this is in the past – the dog then was young. His parents were young.

Domestic details indicate a traditional, homely scene.

The significance of the moment is highlighted for the speaker by a bright light.

Direct speech gives immediacy. We infer that they may also be calling to him from 'the other side', i.e. from beyond the grave.

Present tense makes us feel that this event is happening now, is still happening, and will continue to happen in the present – as if it exists, frozen in the poet's memory.

Very particular and precise details are picked out – as if describing a photograph.

'slowly' and 'Leisurely' (16) seem to slow down the action, as if we are watching it in slow motion.

'I' tells us the poet is there (as a child), but also not there, i.e. he is outside the frame of the picnic scene that he describes.

Eden Rock

They are waiting for me somewhere beyond Eden Rock:
My father, twenty-five, in the same suit
Of Genuine Irish Tweed, his terrier Jack
Still two years old and trembling at his feet.

5 My mother, twenty-three, in a sprigged dress
Drawn at the waist, ribbon in her straw hat,
Has spread the stiff white cloth over the grass.
Her hair, the colour of wheat, takes on the light.

She pours tea from a Thermos, the milk straight
10 From an old H.P. Sauce bottle, a screw
Of paper for a cork; slowly sets out
The same three plates, the tin cups painted blue.

The sky whitens as if lit by three suns.
My mother shades her eyes and looks my way
15 Over the drifted stream. My father spins
A stone along the water. Leisurely,

They beckon to me from the other bank.
I hear them call, 'See where the stream-path is!
Crossing is not as hard as you might think.'

20 I had not thought that it would be like this.

Key: Rhyme   Everyday details   Present tense   Imagery

About the Poem

- The poem was written by Charles Causley (1917–2003). He was brought up in Launceston, between Dartmoor and Bodmin Moor in Cornwall.
- The poem is partly autobiographical. Causley recalls himself as a child on a family picnic with his parents.
- The 'Eden Rock' of the poem is a made-up place. Causley once claimed it was Dartmoor, but confessed 'I have no idea, I made it up!'

Ideas, Themes and Issues

- **Love:** The poet describes his parents, their dog and the details of the picnic with loving nostalgia and affection.
- **Memory and lost innocence:** Details such as the H.P. Sauce bottle (10), the Thermos flask (9) and the tin cups (12) locate the poet's memory in a certain era, when life was simpler and more innocent.
  - Memory is selective and consists of details, such as the pattern on his mother's dress and the terrier's name.
  - His father is in the 'same suit' (2) – the same as what? As the last time the poet saw him? Or is this the suit his father is always wearing, in the poet's memory? Note how the word is repeated, '<u>same</u> three plates' (12).
- **Unease and death:** The final line tells us that the poet is older now, recalling this event in his mind. We can guess that this is a snapshot from a time in his childhood.
  - There is a slight sense of menace, perhaps indicative of other-worldliness – even death – with the mentions of 'three suns' (13) and the sky that 'whitens' (13)

Form, Structure and Language

- Regular **metre** suggests the scene unfolds in an unhurried, almost dream-like way.
- Everyday details are just **juxtaposed** with symbolic descriptions that suggest things are extraordinary.
- The **present tense** creates a sense of immediacy.
- The name 'Eden' means delight and suggests a place of first innocence.

Quick Test

1. What is the significance of the word 'Eden' in the title?
2. How many people are in the poem?
3. Which line tells us that the poet is recalling a memory?

Key Words

Metre
Juxtapose
Present tense

Follower

My father worked with a horse-plough,
His shoulders globed like a full sail strung
Between the shafts and the furrow.
The horse strained at his clicking tongue.

5 An expert. He would set the wing
And fit the bright steel-pointed sock.
The sod rolled over without breaking.
At the headrig, with a single pluck

Of reins, the sweating team turned round
10 And back into the land. His eye
Narrowed and angled at the ground,
Mapping the furrow exactly.

I stumbled in his hob-nailed wake,
Fell sometimes on the polished sod;
15 Sometimes he rode me on his back
Dipping and rising to his plod.

I wanted to grow up and plough,
To close one eye, stiffen my arm.
All I ever did was follow
In his broad shadow round the farm.

20 I was a nuisance, tripping, falling,
Yapping always. But today
It is my father who keeps stumbling
Behind me, and will not go away.

The father's small actions wield great power and control over the horse, plough and the action of ploughing.

This nautical imagery is sustained through the poem, suggesting majesty and stateliness.

Lots of details here that show the poet understands, from watching his father at work, how ploughs are put together.

The epithet for his father is given prominence at the start of a line and verse. What follows is a description of the technical skills his father had.

Shows that the poet feels the team work as one with the land.

'Mapping' shows the precision and technical skills required to plough successfully.

Hob-nails make the boots durable and sturdy. These are fitting boots for his father to wear.

An image of the freshly turned rich earth that shines, as if polished.

Perhaps a sense of regret that he never became what his father was, i.e. a farmer, but only 'ever' followed.

Old people stumble and so do young children. The stumbling is also a metaphor for not following well. Heaney did not follow his father to become a farmer and now his father stumbles to follow him.

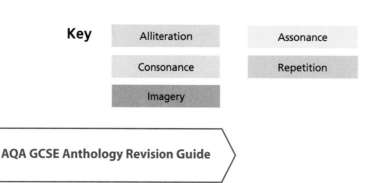

Key	Alliteration	Assonance
	Consonance	Repetition
	Imagery	

About the Poem

- The poem was written by Seamus Heaney about his father, who was a farmer in Northern Ireland.
- The poem describes the hard manual (but very skilled) labour of farming in the days before mechanisation.
- The poet remembers when he was a child and would follow his father as he ploughed the fields. He wanted to grow up to be a farmer like his father, but in the final sentence of the poem their roles are reversed.

Ideas, Themes and Issues

- **Work:** The poet gives a very sensory description of the richness of the land alongside reverence for hard physical graft.
  - The poet details the skilled difficulty of his father's toil as he sweated with his team and admires his father's judgement and skill ('An expert' (5)) when he managed the horse and plough and measured the furrow.
  - It is clear that the poet still has the same respect for farming, as honest toil, that he had when he was a child.
  - The precise details of the ploughing equipment and the process of ploughing have a great impact in the poem, as they clearly did on the child at the time.

- **Relationship between parent and child:** The poet paints his father as a kind of hero. The word 'follower' indicates this.
  - The father's impressive physical presence is described in the phrases 'rode me on his back' (15) and 'broad shadow' (19).
  - The young poet reveres and adores his father, and admires his expertise, precision and power, but recognises that he was a 'nuisance' (20) to his father, unable to keep up and getting in the way, distracting his father with childish chatter.
- **Memory and age:** The sudden shift in the final sentence from the 'then' to 'now' and 'follower' to 'followed', shows how the poet in the present is irritated by his father who, now old, is the one stumblingly following the poet.
  - The phrase 'will not go away' (23) carries a sense of annoyance, but there is also an understanding of the strong bond between father and son.

Form, Structure and Language

- The six regular, four-line verses and regular **rhyme** scheme, combine with the steady **rhythm** to create a sense of the pace and precision of the plough.
- 'Then' and 'now' is contrasted by use of past and present verbs.
- There is heavy use of **alliteration** (e.g. 'strained at his clicking tongue' (4)) which has the effect of mimicking the sound of the horse and plough at work.
- **Assonance** in the fourth verse gives a sense of the pride and reverence that the son has for his father.

Key Words

Rhyme
Rhythm
Alliteration
Assonance

Quick Test

1. Where does the poet set the main part of the poem?
2. Who is in the poem?
3. What did the young poet want to do when he grew up?

Slightly formal in the use of 'mother.' The comma makes us pause and gives it further emphasis.

'acre' is a measurement of area – 'prairies' reinforces the image of vast space in the empty house to suggest that the speaker feels anxious about moving into the house – a big step into adulthood.

The focus shifts here to 'I' (away from 'mother' and 'you').

One of several references to hands (touching, contact and closeness).

Recalls the image of the kite in the second verse.

A measure of space between two points.

'back to base' connects with 'anchor' in line 8, showing the speaker's relationship with his mother.

The image of the measuring tape, with his mother at one end (anchor) and the speaker at the other, (kite) symbolises the history they share. The two single-word 'sentences' stand out in the poem.

An image of the speaker measuring the floor by counting his paces as he moves across it.

Mother, any distance

Mother, any distance greater than a single span
requires a second pair of hands.
You come to help me measure windows, pelmets, doors,
the acres of the walls, the prairies of the floors.

5 You at the zero-end, me with the spool of tape, recording
length, reporting metres, centimetres back to base, then leaving
up the stairs, the line still feeding out, unreeling
years between us. Anchor. Kite.

I space-walk through the empty bedrooms, climb
10 the ladder to the loft, to breaking point, where something
has to give;
two floors below your fingertips still pinch
the last one-hundredth of an inch . . . I reach
towards a hatch that opens on an endless sky
15 to fall or fly.

Key:

Language of space exploration

Precise measurement vocabulary

Metaphor

About the Poem

- The poem was written by Simon Armitage and was first published in 1993. The poem was untitled when published and is now referred to by the first three words of the first line.
- The poem describes the speaker's memory of how his mother helped him take measurements for furnishing his new house. The speaker may be Armitage himself, speaking as a younger man.
- The whole poem is an extended metaphor for the speaker's relationship with his mother and how, while he moves away, they still keep in touch.

Ideas, Themes and Issues

- **Parent-child relationship:** The poem describes the increasing distance between mother and son, symbolised by the measuring tape which she holds at the 'zero-end' (5) while he climbs to the top of the house, measuring as he goes.
  - The poem hints that the speaker feels a bit daunted at moving into the house – perhaps he is leaving home for the first time?
  - The speaker still wants to feel connected to his mother, even as he is taking giant steps (literally and figuratively) to move away from her. The **imagery** of 'Anchor. Kite.' (8) is particularly apt and striking in conveying this relationship.
- **Moving away and connection:** The poem develops the idea of moving away in the sense of becoming an independent adult, but still remaining connected to parents through the extended metaphor of the measuring tape.
  - The language of space exploration ('back to base' (6), and 'space-walk' (9)) humorously compares the speaker's upward exploration of the house to an astronaut's journey into space.
  - The speaker still feels his mother holding tightly ('pinch' (12)) onto the end of the tape, but at the same time he has to 'reach' (13) to the endless sky – towards independence.
- **Distance:** Though the poem was originally untitled, the title by which it is now known, *Mother, any distance* has additional significance beyond its literal use in the poem. It suggests that the speaker will always, on some level, need his mother to be there, no matter what the literal distance between them.

Form, Structure and Language

- The poem starts off with a regular rhyme scheme, but disintegrates into **irregular rhyme** as the poem develops.
- Uneven line lengths are particularly pronounced in the third verse as formality dissolves.
- The form approximates to a **sonnet** – two quatrains (groups of 4 lines) and a sestet (group of 6 lines) with an extra short line at the end, making 15 lines instead of the usual 14.
- The structure of the poem mirrors the speaker's emotions from precise measurement under his mother's eye ('recording' (5), 'reporting' (6) and 'back to base' (6)), which suggest formality and rules, to stretching the tape towards the somewhat scary prospect of independence and freedom ('to fall or fly' (15)).
- It starts out as a formal sonnet, but gradually dissolves into free verse, without rhyme and with uneven line lengths reflecting the speaker's movement towards independence.

Quick Test

1. Who is the speaker of the poem?
2. Who is the speaker addressing in the opening line?
3. What does the speaker do in the final sentence of the poem?

Before You Were Mine

I'm ten years away from the corner you laugh on
with your pals, Maggie McGeeney and Jean Duff.
The three of you bend from the waist, holding
each other, or your knees, and shriek at the pavement.
5 Your polka-dot dress blows round your legs. Marilyn.

I'm not here yet. The thought of me doesn't occur
in the ballroom with the thousand eyes, the fizzy, movie tomorrows
the right walk home could bring. I knew you would dance
like that. Before you were mine, your Ma stands at the close
10 with a hiding for the late one. You reckon it's worth it.

The decade ahead of my loud, possessive yell was the best one, eh?
I remember my hands in those high-heeled red shoes, relics,
and now your ghost clatters toward me over George Square
till I see you, clear as scent, under the tree,
15 with its lights, and whose small bites on your neck, sweetheart?

Cha cha cha! You'd teach me the steps on the way home from Mass,
stamping stars from the wrong pavement. Even then
I wanted the bold girl winking in Portobello, somewhere
in Scotland, before I was born. That glamorous love lasts
20 where you sparkle and waltz and laugh before you were mine.

Side annotations (left):

- References an iconic image of Marilyn Monroe, a 1950s film star, with her skirt blowing up as she stands over an air vent in the street.

- A reference to a 'mirrorball', hung in ballrooms to reflect light.

- The speaker sounds possessive of her mother.

- The sound of her mother's high-heeled shoes on paving stones.

- 'I' appears in every verse, though the speaker is talking about her mother's life.

- Repeats 'before you were mine' from the second verse (and title), emphasising the enduring love between mother and daughter.

Side annotations (right):

- The speaker uses the present tense to describe a scene from the past. The speaker addresses her mother directly.

- The speaker is not yet born (see also the first four words of the poem).

- Talks to her mother as if she knew her well at this time, though she wasn't yet born.

- A reference to the speaker as a baby crying.

- Objects that have survived and have been preserved, often belonging to dead and venerated saints.

- A city square in Glasgow.

- Portobello Beach is an eastern suburb of Edinburgh.

Key:

Imagery	Familiar, conversational language
Images of light	Imagery of sounds

About the Poem

- The poem was written by Carol Ann Duffy in response to an old photograph of her mother as a young woman. Her mother was named Mary. Duffy was born in 1955.

- The speaker (Duffy writing about her mother), imagines her mother's glamorous life before her daughter was born.
- The tone is both admiring and wistful, as the speaker vividly imagines her mother's life as a young woman before motherhood.

Ideas, Themes and Issues

- **Mother–daughter love:** The title is repeated in the poem and suggests something a mother might say to a daughter, but here it is inverted: the daughter says it to the mother.
  - The title speaks of possessiveness and suggests the closeness of their relationship.
  - There is another mother in lines 9–10. This is the speaker's grandmother.
  - The speaker's tone is familiar and affectionate. She romanticises her mother's earlier life in the late 1940s and 1950s.
  - The sense of possession that the speaker feels for her mother is especially clear in the phrase 'I wanted' in line 18. It's almost as if the speaker envies the life her mother had before she herself was born.
- **Time-framing:** The poet speaks as if she knew her mother well in the years before her mother gave birth.
  - There's a reference to her mother's ghost in line 13, but this is the ghost of her mother's younger self.
  - Clever use of the present tense, and the framing the poet uses in lines 1 and line 6, enables the speaker to project herself imaginatively into a time that in reality she could not know.
- **Contrast:** The speaker uses vivid sensory **imagery** of light, colour, sounds and smell to visualise her mother's glamorous, carefree life, where she 'sparkled', before having her daughter.
  - There is a contrast between the mother's earlier life and motherhood, which brought 'my loud, possessive yell' (11).
  - In the third and fourth verses the poet cleverly intertwines real memories of her own childhood with their links to her mother's pre-baby past – the shoes, the scent and dancing.

Form, Structure and Language

- The poem has long sentences interspersed with very short sentences. The short sentences are the speaker's own comments or asides.
- Questions, an exclamation, contractions and vocabulary choices give a **conversational**, intimate and familiar tone.
- The **present tense** indicates the time before the speaker was born. She imaginatively adds detail to memories that her mother has shared and the present tense makes them seem vivid.

> ### Key Point
>
> This is a very intense and unconventional love poem from daughter to mother.

> ### Key Words
>
> Contrast
> Imagery
> Conversational
> Present tense

> ### Quick Test
>
> 1. Who is the 'you' of the poem?
> 2. Who is the 'I'?
> 3. Which era is evoked?

Eden Rock

1 What is the significance of water and streams as symbols in the poem? Tick the correct answer.

A symbols of sadness ☐ **C** symbols of distance ☐

B symbols of death ☐ **D** symbols of dreams ☐ [1]

2 Identify three domestic details in the poem.

....

.... [3]

3 Pick out all the references to clothes and appearance in the poem.

....

.... [3]

4 What is the significance of the final line?

.... [1]

5 What do you think is suggested by the phrases 'the sky whitens' and 'three suns' (13)? Complete the sentence below.

The poet uses the phrases 'the sky whitens' and 'three suns' to indicate a) ....

and b) .... [2]

6 Identify three ways the poet makes us understand that they are describing a memory.

....

.... [3]

7 How do we know that the poet is in the poem?

.... [1]

8 Identify the rhyme scheme used in the poem.

.... [1]

9 Which words in the poem seem to slow down the action?

.... [1]

10 Which tense is mainly used in the poem? What is the effect of this?

....

.... [2]

Follower

1 What does the poet most admire about his father? Tick the correct answer.

A his stumbling ☐ **C** his abilities as a ploughman ☐

B his farm ☐ **D** his physique ☐ [1]

2 Identify three details from verses 1–4 about the ploughing process.

.... [3]

3 Find three examples of imagery in the poem.

.... [3]

4 What is the effect of the different tenses used in the poem?

.... [1]

5 The poet uses verbs to show that ploughing is hard physical work. Identify three of them.

.... [3]

6 Identify three ways the poet makes us understand that he is describing a memory.

.... [3]

7 In what ways is the poet a 'follower' of his father?

....

.... [2]

8 Identify the rhyme scheme used in the poem.

.... [1]

9 Which sounds seem to mimic the sounds of a clicking tongue?

.... [1]

10 What is the significance of the word 'stumbling' in the final verse?

....

....

.... [2]

Mother, any distance

1 What situation does the poem describe?

.... [1]

2 What is the name given to the poetic technique that the poet uses in the whole poem?

.... [1]

3 Why does the speaker refer to themselves using images of space exploration? What do these suggest about their feelings at this time?

....

....

.... [2]

4 Pick out two references to large spaces in the first quatrain. What do these suggest about the speaker's new house?

.... [2]

5 The words, 'Anchor. Kite.' (8) refer to whom?

....

6 How does the space between mother and son change as the poem develops? How is the idea of connection retained?

....

....

.... [2]

7 Pick out an image that suggests that the mother is keen to hold a connection with her son.

.... [1]

8 What does the final line of the poem suggest about the speaker's feelings?

.... [1]

9 In what ways does the structure of the poem reinforce its content?

....

.... [1]

10 Apart from being the first three words of the first line, what other significance might the title of the poem have?

.... [1]

Before You Were Mine

1. How is the sense of a different era evoked in the first verse?

[2]

2. How many years before the speaker's own birth was the photograph taken?

[1]

3. Which two specific memories link the speaker with her mother's life before she was born?

[2]

4. How many years before the speaker's own birth did the scene in the first verse take place?

[2]

5. What is the effect of the repeated phrase, 'before you were mine'?

[1]

6. In what sense could the relationship in the poem be described as unconventional?

[1]

7. Find two images in the second verse that the speaker uses to create a romanticised view of their mother's previous life.

[2]

8. What is suggested by the word 'wrong' in the phrase 'stamping stars from the wrong pavement.' (17)?

[2]

9. There are two questions in the poem. Who do you think speaks them and what is unusual about this?

[2]

10. In the line 'That glamorous love lasts' (19), what might the speaker be suggesting about the relationship between mother and daughter?

[1]

Neutral Tones

1   Tick the correct answer. The poem describes:

   A   a real event   ☐   **C**   a conversation   ☐

   B   a recurring memory   ☐   **D**   all of the above   ☐   [1]

2   Where does the scene in the poem take place?

    [1]

3   What season does the poem take place in?

    [1]

4   What do you think the two people in the poem say to each other?

    [2]

5   How does the poet describe his ex-lover's eyes?

    [2]

6   Complete the quotation:

   'Alive enough to have _____ to die'   [1]

7   Which word best describes the tone of the poem? Circle the correct answer.

   hopeful   **cheerful**   **dreamlike**   **nostalgic**   **bleak**   [1]

8   Why do you think the sun is described as 'God-curst'?

    [1]

9   How do we know this event took place in the past? Give TWO reasons.

    [2]

10   Give one example of alliteration in the poem. Say what effect this has.

    [2]

The Farmer's Bride

1 In what ways does the punctuation used in the poem imitate natural speech? Give two examples.

.... [2]

2 Based on the evidence given in the poem, do you think the farmer and his bride are mismatched? Give three examples from the poem as evidence for your answer.

.... [3]

3 The farmer uses dialect – his own natural speech. Find three examples of this in the poem.

.... [3]

4 Which phrase in the poem shows that the farmer is confused by his wife's behaviour?

.... [1]

5 What is the word for a poem that has one speaker who is not the poet, like this one?

.... [1]

6 Which of the following words best describe the farmer? Circle the correct answer. [1]

understanding   **loving**   **unfaithful**   **callous**   **confused**

7 What do we learn about the status of women in this community?

....

.... [1]

8 What does the poet's use of enjambment and caesura indicate about the wife's emotional state?

.... [1]

9 Find two examples of direct speech in the poem. What is the effect of these?

....

....

.... [2]

10 Comment on the repetition and internal rhyme of the final three lines. How are these lines different from the rest of the poem?

....

.... [1]

Walking Away

1 Where and when does the incident in the poem take place?

.... [2]

2 What is the significance of the title of the poem?

.... [1]

3 Find a description in the first verse that suggests change is in the air.

.... [1]

4 What does the simile in lines 4–5 indicate about the relationship?

....

....

.... [2]

5 What does the image 'half-fledged' (8) suggest about **a)** the son and **b)** the speaker's emotions?

....

....

....

.... [2]

6 'Drifting away' (5) and 'eddying away' (11) suggest that the speaker feels his son is: (choose two)

A certain ☐   **C** vulnerable ☐

B purposeless ☐   **D** determined ☐ [2]

7 Why does the poet use the word 'Gnaws' (17) to describe a memory that won't go away? What is the effect of this word?

....

....

....

.... [2]

8 Identify two words that indicate that the poet is struggling to express an idea.

.... [2]

Letters from Yorkshire

1 What sort of 'news' does he send from Yorkshire?

[1]

2 Why do you think he writes letters rather than email or texts?

[1]

3 Why do you think the poet changes pronouns from 'his' and 'he' to 'you'?

[1]

4 How important to the speaker are the letters that he sends?

[1]

5 When the speaker says 'that other world' (12) what is being referred to?

[1]

6 Does the speaker think her work and lifestyle is less meaningful than 'his'? Give your reasons.

[2]

7 What does the word 'our' in the final line suggest about the nature of their relationship?

[1]

8 What is the effect of the poet's use of present participles ('feeding', 'pouring', 'turning', 'digging')?

[1]

9 At what point in the poem does the speaker speak on 'his' behalf?

[1]

10 Despite living at a distance from each other, this relationship remains a close one. How does the poet convey this in the poem?

[2]

Winter Swans

The clouds had given their all –
two days of rain and then a break
in which we walked,

> There has been a storm which is now over.

the waterlogged earth
5 gulping for breath at our feet
as we skirted the lake, silent and apart,

> This has two meanings – to go around the edge and to avoid an issue.

> Indicates a rift in their relationship.

until the swans came and stopped us
with a show of tipping in unison.
As if rolling weights down their bodies to their heads

> The swans are in harmony: 'unison' means simultaneously and 'tipping' describes them lowering their heads to the water.

10 they halved themselves in the dark water,
icebergs of white feather, paused before returning again
like boats righting in rough weather.

> Icebergs are hard and feathers soft, so the image is strikingly incongruous.

> Compares swans to capsized boats as they dip under the water then re-emerge. Suggests that swans have the ability to right themselves; so maybe the couple can too?

'They mate for life' you said as they left,
porcelain over the stilling water. I didn't reply
15 but as we moved on through the afternoon light,

> A second image of hardness for the swans.

slow-stepping in the lake's shingle and sand,
I noticed our hands, that had, somehow,
swum the distance between us

> Compare 'skirted' in line 6. Now they're moving together, slowly.

and folded, one over the other,
20 like a pair of wings settling after flight

> This image links the couple's hands with the swans and is continued in the final couplet and its simile.

> 'stilling' used as an adjective is unusual. We would usually expect 'still', but stilling gives an added sense of 'becoming calm and still'; i.e. not yet 'still'.

Key:

Simile	Personification	Alliteration
Imagery	Consonance	

About the Poem

- The poem was written by Owen Sheers and published in his collection *Skirrid Hill* in 2005.
- The poem explores the relationship between two lovers, symbolised by an observation of swans on a lake in winter.
- The poem describes one incident, written from one person's point of view.
- The speaker may be male or female.

Ideas, Themes and Issues

- **Reconciliation:** Swans are traditionally seen as monogamous birds (13). The couple eventually both make a connection between the swans' relationship and their own.
  - Initially, something about the swans stopped the couple as they walked: the way that the swans moved in a synchronised way together. They modeled a picture of harmony, peace and togetherness, showing the couple that reconciliation might be possible.
  - The swans leave and the couple walk on, but this time with hands held 'like a pair of wings settling after flight' (20). The simile calls back to the swans and the lesson the couple have taken from observing them.
  - The final line holds out the possibility for renewal in their relationship, but the line isn't punctuated, suggesting that this might be a start at renewal, but it's not certain if they will reconcile or not.
- **Nature:** The speaker uses the natural setting of a lake in winter to subtly suggest what has been going on in the relationship – there has been a storm and the earth is 'waterlogged' (4).
  - The details we are given of the 'stilling water' (14) (gradually growing still) after the swans depart, the afternoon light and their slowed pace, combine to give a sense that calm has grown between the two of them after witnessing the swans.
  - The sense of a growing calmness leads up to that final image of the hands moving together, like swan's wings, broaching the distance and disharmony that had been between them at the start of their walk.

Form, Structure and Language

- There is no full stop at the end of the final line, as if the poem is to be continued.
- Images of nature are used to convey feelings in a relationship.
- Consonance (e.g. 'righting in rough' (12); 'shingle and sand' (16); 'somehow, /swum' (17-18')) suggest that the harmony shown by the swans has a harmonising effect on the couple.
- Alliteration of 's' in lines 6 and 7 emphasises the silence that exists between them.

Key Words

Simile
Consonance
Alliteration

Quick Test

1. Where is the poem set?
2. What time of year is it?
3. What do the couple observe on their walk?

The name Singh is used by Sikh men.

Singh Song!

I run just one ov my daddy's shops
from 9 o'clock to 9 o'clock
and he vunt me not to hav a break
but ven nobody in, I do di lock –

She means more to him than the shop.

5   cos up di stairs is my newly bride
vee share in chapatti
vee share in di chutney
after vee hav made luv
like vee rowing through Putney –

'Putney' is Punjabi for 'wife' and is also an area of London.

10   Ven I return vid my pinnie untied
di shoppers always point and cry:

Ties in with the title of the poem.

Hey Singh, ver yoo bin?
Yor lemons are limes
yor bananas are plantain,
15   *dis dirty little floor need a little bit of mop*
in di worst Indian shop
on di whole Indian road –

The road is separate from the rest of the community.

Above my head high heel tap di ground
as my vife on di web is playing wid di mouse

Suggests a 'cat and mouse' game – the wife is in the position of power.

20   ven she netting two cat on her Sikh lover site
she book dem for di meat at di cheese ov
     her price –

my bride

Links her culture with unexpected behaviour.

she effing at my mum
in all di colours of Punjabi
den stumble like a drunk
25   making fun at my daddy

my bride

Contrasting images of danger and comfort.

tiny eyes ov a gun
and di tummy ov a teddy

my bride
30 she hav a red crew cut
and she wear a Tartan sari

Mix of Western and Indian styles.

a donkey jacket and some pumps
on di squeak ov di girls dat are pinching my
    sweeties –

Ven I return from di tickle ov my bride

Metaphor for sex.

35 di shoppers always point and cry:
Hey Singh, ver yoo bin?
Di milk is out ov date
and di bread is alvays stale,
di tings yoo hav on offer yoo hav never got in stock
40 *in di worst Indian shop*
on di whole Indian road –

Late in di midnight hour
ven yoo shoppers are wrap up quiet
ven di precinct is concrete-cool

Alliteration and metaphor show how the couple add romance to a bland setting.

45 vee cum down whispering stairs
and sit on my silver stool,
from behind di chocolate bars
vee stare past di half-price window signs
at di beaches ov di UK in di brightey moon

The play on words is caused by the similarity to 'Blighty' – a word often used for Britain. It comes from the Hindi word for 'foreign'.

50 from di stool each night she say,
How much do yoo charge for dat moon baby?

from di stool each night I say,
Is half di cost ov yoo baby,

A corny romantic line.

from di stool each night she say,
55 *How much does dat come to baby?*

A personal ritual.

from di stool each night I say,
Is priceless baby –

There is no doubting her value to him.

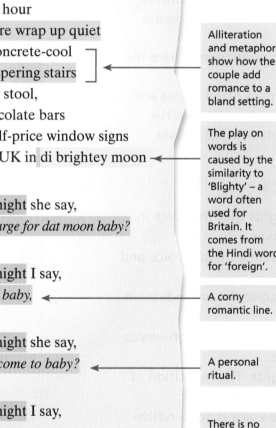

Key:

Contrasting images

Metaphor

Play on words

Repetition

Italics

Grammatical errors

About the Poem

- The poem was written by Daljit Nagra in 1966.
- The poem is a **dramatic monologue**.
- We hear the voice of a Sikh man who works in his father's shop. He describes his daily routine, problems and dreams.
- The man is recently married to an unconventional Sikh wife. Both seem dissatisfied with life and spend their evenings dreaming together.
- Through his descriptions of others he reveals aspects of himself.

Ideas, Themes and Issues

- **Racism:** The customers are overly critical of the man, his shop and his goods, and label his shop as 'Indian'.
- **Alienation and assimilation:** The Indian community is distinct from the rest of the neighbourhood. The wife's clothes and the things she does are a mix of two cultures.
- **Modern urban lives:** The precinct and shop are mundane and unromantic.
- **Clashing generations:** The man and his wife don't share the same values as his parents.
- **Sexual desire, passion and love:** The man often thinks about his wife and takes every opportunity to be with her. His desire for her and pleasure in their relationship is clear.

Form, Structure and Language

- Use of non-standard grammar highlights that the voice in the poem is not a native English speaker.
- **Idiolect** and **non-standard English** create a unique voice and shows that this is a personal story.
- Contrasting images and **metaphors** suggest the unpredictable nature of the wife.
- The boisterous and playful tone, rhymes and play-on-words reflect the personalities of the couple.
- The wife is always in the man's thoughts. The repetition of the **possessive pronoun** 'my' shows his pride in her.
- Grammatical errors highlight that the voice is not a native English speaker.
- The use of italics for the customers' voices emphasises the regularity of their complaints and seems chorus-like.

Key Words

Dramatic monologue
Idiolect
Non-standard English
Metaphor
Possessive pronoun

Quick Test

1. How do we know that the wife is unpredictable?
2. What is the effect of the change in metre and rhyme of the final section?
3. Why do you think the poem is called 'Singh Song!'?
4. What is the effect of the repeated chorus of customers' voices?

The grandfather's clothes (brogues) and body parts are referenced throughout the poem as staging posts on the child's climb.

The grandfather's body is presented in terms of geological features.

The grandfather's age and past working life are indicated: wrinkles, loose skin and soft white hair are mentioned later on.

The child stops to kiss his grandfather as he makes his way to the top.

The image suggests the child's joy at reaching the top.

Climbing my Grandfather

I decide to do it free, without a rope or net.
First, the old brogues, dusty and cracked;
an easy scramble onto his trousers,
pushing into the weave, trying to get a grip.
5 By the overhanging shirt I change
direction, traverse along his belt
to an earth-stained hand. The nails
are splintered and give good purchase,
the skin of his finger is smooth and thick
10 like warm ice. On his arm I discover
the glassy ridge of a scar, place my feet
gently in the old stitches and move on.
At his firm shoulder, I rest for a while
in the shade, not looking down,
15 for climbing has its dangers, then pull
myself up the loose skin of his neck
to a smiling mouth to drink among teeth.
Refreshed, I cross the screed cheek,
to stare into his brown eyes, watch a pupil
20 slowly open and close. Then up over
the forehead, the wrinkles well-spaced
and easy, to his thick hair (soft and white
at this altitude), reaching for the summit,
where gasping for breath I can only lie
25 watching clouds and birds circle,
feeling his heat, knowing
the slow pulse of his good heart.

Speaker uses present tense, first-person.

'dusty and cracked' suggests the grandfather's age and experience; also suggests the earth at the foot of a mountain.

Traverse means to cross sideways.

Purchase here means grip.

'warm ice' is a paradoxical image that brings together the child's love for his grandfather with the image of the mountain that he is using for him.

The rhythm of the line conveys the sound of the heartbeat.

Key: Extended metaphor   Metaphor   Simile   Preposition

Poem Overviews 4: Climbing My Grandfather

About the Poem

- The poem was written by Andrew Waterhouse, who grew up in Scarborough and lived in Northumbria.
- In the poem, the speaker, who may be the poet himself, recalls how as a child he would crawl over his grandfather and likens this to an explorer climbing a mountain.
- The poem may be autobiographical, but it is a memory many people would have, or would strongly identify with.

Ideas, Themes and Issues

- **Family love:** The **extended metaphor** of mountaineering to describe a child crawling slowly up the body of his grandfather is touching and humorous.
  - As the grandfather allows the child to climb up his clothes and body, and to the top of his head, he shows tolerance, patience and love.
  - The child sees the climb as a challenge and potentially dangerous, so he takes his time.
- **A challenging climb:** The child likens his grandfather to a mountain – imposing and solid, but also offering some easy patches for the child to climb – 'easy scramble' (3) and 'give good purchase' (8) show this.
  - The grandfather doesn't offer help to the child – he allows him to find his own way through the challenges.
  - Throughout the poem the grandfather is presented as a friendly mountain ('smiling mouth' (17), 'soft and white' (22)) offering landmarks to the climber along the way until he reaches the 'summit' (23) – his head.

> ### Key Point
>
> The poem uses an extended metaphor of climbing a mountain to represent a child climbing his grandfather.

- **Respect:** Though the child climbs all over his grandfather, the poem indicates that he has respect for him. Not only is he huge compared to the child, and old, but the child is also aware of taking risks ('for climbing has its dangers' (15)).
  - The child's determination is shown in the first line, 'I decide' and his own bravery in attempting to climb his older relative is indicated by 'do it free, without a rope or net'.
  - There's a suggestion that his grandfather is a formidable figure to the child. He places his feet 'gently' (12), so as not to disturb him too much.

Form, Structure and Language

- The sentences divide up the child's climb into stages.
- **Prepositions** that indicate time or position 'First', 'by', 'at', 'then' are carefully used to show his progress as he climbs.
- One single extended verse, regular line length and unrhymed: the sentence punctuation is used to suggest breaks and pauses and the rhythm of the climb in one long sequence.
- Uses an extended metaphor that likens the child's climb to a mountaineer climbing a mountain.
- The **simile** 'like warm ice' (10) encapsulates the idea that the grandfather is a metaphorical mountain to the child.

Quick Test
1. What happens in the poem?
2. Who is 'I'?
3. What does the speaker feel when he reaches the top?

Key Words
Extended metaphor
Prepositions
Simile

Winter Swans

1 What are swans often seen as being representatives of?

_____ [1]

2 What has the weather been like, earlier?

_____ [1]

3 What parallel does the poet draw between the relationship of the couple and the state of the earth?

_____

_____ [1]

4 What two things does the speaker notice about the way the swans move?

_____

_____ [2]

5 Which words tell you that the swans have left calm behind them when they depart?

_____ [1]

6 Though swans are softly feathered and warm, the poet uses two images of hard coldness to describe them. What are the images?

_____ [2]

7 Why do you think the speaker does not reply when his partner says, 'They mate for life' (13)?

_____

_____ [1]

8 What is the mood and atmosphere at the end? Which words tell you this?

_____

_____ [2]

9 What does the speaker notice at the end of the poem?

_____ [1]

10 How does the poet link the couple's reconciliation back to the swans in the final line?

_____ [1]

Singh Song!

1 In what way is the title a pun or play on words?

_____

_____ [1]

2 What does the speaker's use of non-standard English tell us about him?

_____ [1]

3 What is the name given to this form of poetry in which we hear the voice of one speaker?

_____ [1]

4 What is the effect of the image of the wife playing with the mouse?

_____ [1]

5 In the ninth verse, why does the couple spend time looking out at the moon?

_____

_____ [1]

6 Why does the poet choose to repeat the line, 'Hey Singh, ver yoo bin?'

_____ [1]

7 Give two examples that show the wife is rebelling against tradition.

_____

_____ [2]

8 Give two examples that show the wife is following tradition.

_____

_____ [2]

9 What is the effect of the repeated phrase 'my bride'?

_____

_____ [1]

10 Why is it fitting that the poem ends with a conversation about how much things cost?

_____

_____ [2]

Climbing My Grandfather

1 What does the speaker imagine his grandfather is in the poem?

.... [1]

2 What decision does the speaker make before he starts?

.... [1]

3 What do the grandfather's clothes and body parts become for the speaker?

.... [1]

4 How does the speaker feel about the climb? How does he feel about his grandfather?

....

....

.... [2]

5 Name two qualities that his grandfather and the mountain have in common.

....

.... [2]

6 Which lines tell you that the speaker has respect for his grandfather?

.... [1]

7 How does the structure of the poem mirror the climb?

....

.... [1]

8 How does the child feel when he reaches the top?

.... [1]

9 In the line 'to a smiling mouth to drink among teeth' (17), what is the child doing?

.... [1]

10 In what way does the final line sound like its meaning?

.... [1]

Eden Rock

1 How many people are on the picnic?

_____ [1]

2 What does the poem describe? Tick the correct answer.

A a real event ☐   **C** a dream ☐

B a memory ☐   **D** all of the above ☐   [1]

3 Pick out two symbols in the poem and analyse their effects.

_____

_____ [2]

4 'See where the stream-path is!/Crossing is not as hard as you might think.' (18–19). What is the effect of these lines?

_____ [1]

5 Why does the poet include so many visual details in the poem?

_____ [1]

6 Complete the summary.

a) The poem shows that the poet feels great _____ for his parents.

b) The poet is older now and feels _____ from his parents. [2]

7 Which word best describes the tone of the poem?

thoughtful   **sad**   **mysterious**   **nostalgic**   **dramatic**   [1]

8 Why do you think the terrier is 'trembling'?

_____ [1]

9 What is the effect of the use of the present tense in the poem?

_____ [1]

10 'I had not thought that it would be like this.' (20). Comment on the significance of this line for the poem as a whole.

_____

_____ [2]

Follower

1 In what ways is the title 'Follower' appropriate for this poem?

_____

_____ [2]

2 Identify one image in the first verse that shows the father is a powerful man.

_____ [1]

3 How do we know the memory in this poem happened a long time ago?

_____

_____ [2]

4 What did the poet hope to inherit from his father? Tick the correct answer. [1]

  A his plough ☐   **C** his physique ☐

  B his farming skills ☐   **D** his shadow ☐

5 How do we know the poet has great technical knowledge of ploughing?

_____

_____ [1]

6 Which of the following words does Heaney use to talk about the field? Tick the correct answers.

  A sod ☐   **C** earth ☐

  B ground ☐   **D** land ☐ [2]

7 Which words tell us that ploughing is a very precise art?

_____ [3]

8 Where in the poem does Heaney tell us that he wanted to be like his father?

_____ [1]

9 Identify the word where the poem shifts from 'then' to 'now'.

_____ [1]

10 The poet calls himself as a child a 'nuisance' (20). Does he now feel the same way about his father?

_____

_____ [2]

Mother, any distance

1 What is the poem mainly about? Tick the correct answer.

A love as 'letting go' ☐　　C moving home ☐

B measurement ☐　　D choosing new furnishings ☐ [1]

2 Which poetic form does the poet use, loosely, in this poem?

.... [1]

3 In your view, is this poem a love poem? Explain your answer.

....

....

.... [2]

4 What is suggested by the lines, 'the line still feeding out, unreeling/ years between us' (7–8)?

.... [1]

5 Why does the speaker choose to start by referring to metric measurements and then change to imperial?

....

....

.... [1]

6 What does the poet use to symbolise the growing distance, yet connection, between mother and son?

.... [1]

7 What might be the significance of the word 'hatch' in line 14?

....

.... [1]

8 Pick out two words in the poem that suggest the mother represents safety to the speaker.

.... [2]

9 At the end of the poem, the speaker reaches towards something. What is he reaching for? Suggest two things.

.... [2]

10 Which image in the poem does the final line link back to?

.... [1]

Before You Were Mine

1 How does the speaker manage to include herself in descriptions of her mother's life before she was born?

.... [1]

2 Whose ghost does the speaker see?

.... [1]

3 Whose mother is mentioned in the poem, apart from the speaker's?

.... [1]

4 What is the effect of the references to Hollywood films in the poem?

.... [1]

5 What might the 'ballroom with the thousand eyes' (7) refer to?

....

.... [2]

6 Which phrase suggests that perhaps the mother's life did not turn out as she expected?

.... [1]

7 How would you describe the tone of the poem? Choose one of these words, or come up with your own adjective. Explain your choice.

wistful   **nostalgic**   **hopeful**   **exuberant**

....

.... [2]

8 Why might the speaker ask whether the years before she was born were the best years of her mother's life?

.... [1]

9 Where is the poem mainly set?

.... [1]

10 What is the effect of the speaker's use of the present tense in the poem?

.... [1]

Winter Swans

1 What central natural image does the poet use in this poem?

.... [1]

2 How does the poet describe the earth after the storm?

.... [1]

3 What do swans symbolise for the 'you' of the poem?

.... [1]

4 Which words indicate that there has been a rift in the relationship?

.... [1]

5 What do the swans 'show' the couple?

.... [1]

6 Which image indicates that the swans are capable of making things right after trouble?

.... [1]

7 What are two possible meanings of the word 'skirted' (6) and how are both applicable here?

....

.... [2]

8 What does the lack of punctuation in the final verse suggest?

....

.... [1]

9 What does 'slow-stepping' (16) tell us about the relationship?

.... [1]

10 How do the held hands in the final verse link back to the central natural image?

.... [2]

Singh Song!

1 What does the speaker do for a living?

.... [1]

2 What do the physical descriptions of his wife in the sixth verse reveal about the speaker's feelings for her?

.... [1]

3 In what way does the structure of the poem resemble a song?

.... [1]

4 Find two examples of puns or word play in the poem.

.... [2]

5 Which of the following words best describes the tone of the poem? [1]

severe   **comical**   **bitter**   **nostalgic**   **critical**

6 Where is the shop situated?

.... [1]

7 In what three ways does his wife offer the husband escape from his mundane existence?

....

....

.... [3]

8 What does the use of a pun (Singh/sing) in the title suggest about the tone of the poem?

.... [1]

9 What does the poet's use of italics in the final eight lines suggest?

....

.... [1]

10 What is Singh's attitude towards his customers? What makes you think so?

....

.... [1]

Climbing My Grandfather

1 In what ways does the structure of the poem contribute to its meaning?

....

.... [2]

2 Which details tell you about the grandfather's life experiences?

.... [1]

3 Give two examples of phrases that tell you the grandfather is benevolent to the child during his climb.

.... [1]

4 Does the child feel nervous during the climb?

....

.... [1]

5 What does the child see at the summit? How is this humorous?

....

.... [2]

6 Why would the grandfather have skin like 'warm ice' (10) to the child?

.... [1]

7 Why do you think the child decides to climb without a rope or safety net?

.... [2]

8 What is the effect of the poet's use of present tense in the poem?

.... [1]

9 Pick out the sequence words that the poet uses to indicate the stages of the climb.

.... [4]

10 Find two details in which the poet likens the grandfather to a geological feature.

....

.... [2]

Poem Analysis: Comparing Poems

Understanding the Question

- In the exam you will be asked to compare two poems from the anthology cluster you have studied.
- The question will ask you to compare a named poem, which will be printed on the paper, with another poem of your choice from the same cluster.
- A list of all the poems in the cluster will be printed for you as a reminder but you will not have them in front of you.
- Therefore, you must make sure you know all the poems really well so you can write a good comparison answer.
- Your answer needs to include:
  - Your understanding and response to the poems.
  - Textual references (quotations or paraphrases) that support your interpretations.
  - Appropriate use of subject terminology.
  - Analysis of the language, form and structure of the poems.
  - Analysis of the poets' methods and how they use them to achieve meanings and effects.
  - Reference to, and understanding of, the relationships between poems and the contexts in which they were written.
- The question will usually start with the word 'Compare' and a poem from the cluster will be specified in the question. You must use this as one of the poems in your comparison. You then need to choose another poem from the cluster for your comparison.
- Make sure the poem you choose for your second comparison poem is suitable for the exam question.
- You will have no choice of question, so it is important that the poem you choose has enough similarity and difference with the given poem, and is appropriate for the question.
- For example, look at this question:

> Compare the ways that poets present ideas about love that has failed in 'Neutral Tones' and **one** other poem from 'Love and Relationships'.

- You will always be asked to write about the poets' **presentation**. This means you must show understanding of the poets' methods: structure, language choice, techniques, tone and attitude.
- Be aware that you can talk about the ideas and theme of the poem, but this alone will not earn you high marks.
- Examiners are looking for a sophisticated **analysis** and exploration of poetic methods and their effects.
- Students who offer different personal interpretations will also be highly rewarded.

Key Point

Remember that you will only have the named poem in front of you, so make sure you know all the poems really well.

Key Point

Examiners want to see detailed analysis and explanation of poetic techniques and their effects.

Using Comparison Grids

- When you are revising, it may be helpful to use comparison grids to organise your ideas about the poems side by side. Decide on two poems to compare at a time.
- The grid might look like this:

Question focus: e.g. Poets' presentation of love that has failed.		
	Poem 1	**Poem 2**
Themes and ideas – similar – different		
Structure and form – similar – different		
Language features (imagery, repetition, interesting word choices, alliteration, etc.) – similar – different		
Tone and attitude – similar – different		
Personal response and interpretations		

> **Key Point**
>
> Using a comparison grid can be especially helpful when revising the poems.

- Remember that your comparison must consider similarities and differences. You do not need to talk about both of these equally, but you must always be comparing both poems.
- A very common error is to talk about one poem in detail and make only passing mention of the other poem. Plan well, so you have plenty to write about for both poems.
- In the exam, you may prefer to **annotate** (underline or highlight) parts of the poem given in the question with comparison points for your second poem written alongside.
- This can work well, but it's a good idea to use a comparison grid similar to the one above when you are practising comparison answers. It helps you get into the habit of organising your ideas under the right headings.

> **Key Point**
>
> It is vital that you remember to write about both poems, comparing their similarities and differences in relation to the question. Do not talk about just one poem in detail.

> **Key Words**
>
> Presentation
> Analysis
> Annotate

Poem Analysis: Comparing Poems

Planning Your Answer

- In the exam you should allow yourself 10–12 minutes for gathering your ideas and writing your plan.
- Here is a template of a plan:

Introduction	Always state the titles (and poets) that you intend to compare. Always mention the focus of the question to show you are aware of it. Show that you are setting out to write in a comparative way.
Main paragraphs	Include at least three paragraphs. You should have at least three clear points of comparison to make – more, if you have more ideas! Make sure you include references to the poems and use quotations to support your points.
Conclusion	Sum up your main ideas, mention the question focus again and give a personal response to the poems.

Key Point

Planning your answer is important, so spend the recommended time creating your plan.

- Your plan might look like this:

Introduction	Views and ideas about love that has failed: Neutral Tones and When We Two Parted. Similarities – both show speaker's bitterness that love doesn't last; the failure of a past love affair continues to have repercussions for both.
Main paragraphs	**1.** Similar themes/attitudes: speakers have both been hurt by the break up of an affair. Both use the first-person – this makes it more immediate/direct. Note the use of tense in both which links the *then* to *now*. ('Since then, keen lessons …' Hardy; 'the warning of what I feel now', Byron). **2.** Language and effects: Use of neutral colours (white, gray) and sombre natural images ('like an ominous bird'; 'God-curst sun') by Hardy evokes disenchanted mood; similar colours by Byron and formal structure (strong rhythm/rhyme/repetition/patterning 'silence and tears') gives more passionate/angry tone? Both use first-person which makes it more direct. Note the use of tense in both – this links the *then* to *now*. **3.** Different contexts – Hardy's personal; Byron's more veiled in references ('shudder', 'in secret we met') as the lover in question held a place in society.
Conclusion	Both grim and bitter attitude to failure of love affair; both feel wronged, continue to feel effects. Byron more bitter/angry; Hardy more sorrowful.

Writing Your Answer

- When it comes to writing a good comparative essay, there are certain words and phrases that will come in very useful as a way of organising your thoughts to make it easy for the examiner to follow your writing.
- Some useful phrases are:
  - 'Both... however' – this helps you to mention points of similarity followed by difference. For example:

    Both poets use rhyme to suggest control, however in Byron's poem it also suggests cold anger ...

  - 'Although ...' – you could use this when you want to highlight a difference, or contrast, between two poems. For example: '

    Although in Hardy's poem the sensory imagery is cold and colourless, in Duffy's poem it is full of colour, sound and scent.

- Other useful phrases to make links are shown below:

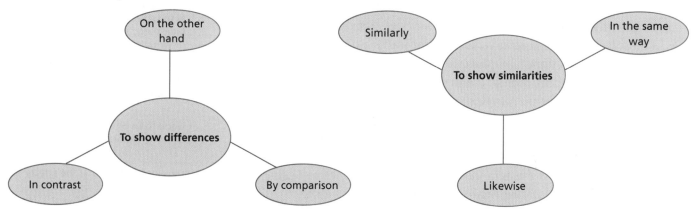

On the other hand

To show differences

In contrast

By comparison

Similarly

To show similarities

In the same way

Likewise

Poem Analysis:
Sample Worked Question and Answer

Sample Worked Question and Answer

Compare how poets present attitudes towards the end of a romantic relationship in 'When We Two Parted' and in **one** other poem from 'Love and relationships'. *(30 marks)*

In 'When We Two Parted', Byron explores the poet's feelings about an affair that has turned out badly. The poet uses a strict poetic structure with tightly controlled rhyme and metre to convey his feelings of bitterness and anger. In Hardy's poem 'Neutral Tones' the poet also presents his feelings about a relationship that has ended. Hardy presents his feelings in the context of the description of a cold, grey winter's day, drawing parallels between that natural scene and the couple's lack of feelings for each other.

Both poets present their attitudes through the poems that are tightly structured and controlled. In Hardy's poem there are four verses of four lines each and he uses a regular rhyme scheme of four beats per line. This gives a sense of detachment and control on the part of the speaker, but also sorrow. As with the poet's feelings, which are 'neutral', like the colours, and as in the title, the rhyme scheme is also 'neutral' and regular. We sense the speaker's feelings of resignation mixed with regret as he recalls that day. In contrast, Byron's poem, though it also uses a very regular and tightly controlled structure, rhythm and rhyme, has a different effect. It suggests the poet's anger and bitterness. There are two beats per line and the beats stress particular words, deliberately: 'in SILence and TEARS / HALF broken– HEARTed / to SEVer for YEARS'. Thus the poet gives the impression of 'spitting' out the words, almost as if he is furious. This is a very different tonal effect from the Hardy poem, which is more gentle (though no less bitter).

The poets' use of colour and imagery of cold is also strikingly similar, though different in key aspects. In Byron's poem, he uses 'pale', 'cold', 'chill', 'colder' and 'shudder' to indicate how their feelings cooled for each other. Nevertheless, we feel as we read on that he feels furious anger at how the affair still affects him now – in other words, he feels resentment that this woman still has power over him. Hardy's use of colour is similar to Byron's in that he uses it to suggest the feelings surrounding the end of a relationship and how feelings cooled between the couple. He refers to a 'white' sun and 'gray', dead leaves to symbolise the death of their love. However, Hardy takes the references to nature further, with images of a 'starving sod' and an 'ominous bird' that further underlines the way that nature echoes and reflects the couple's feelings.

Both poets use 'I' and 'you' to refer to the couples in the poems and both use past and present tense to compare how they feel 'now' with how they felt 'then'. Neither seem to have been able to move on from the relationship that ended years before: Byron because the woman is still active in society and he is often reminded of the affair by hearing

Clear introduction which tells the examiner which poems you will cover and refers closely to the question.

Refers to poets' methods with textual references.

Analysis of writers' methods with subject terminology used judiciously; exploration of effects of writer's methods on reader.

Shows excellent understanding of the poem.

Good focus on structure and detailed exploration of language.

Develops and explores the effects of writers' methods on reader.

Analysis of writers' methods with subject terminology used judiciously; exploration of effects of writer's methods on reader.
Offers an interpretation using a critical style.

Critical, exploratory comparison; judicious use of precise references to support interpretations.

Point, evidence, analysis.

Judicious use of precise references to support and illustrate interpretations.

Critical, exploratory comparison of the two poems.

Thoughtful response and clear link made between poems.

her name – and indeed, they may meet again someday, in different circumstances. In Hardy's case, the poem was written about an unnamed woman who is scarcely described in the poem. The scene at the pond is etched in his memory. 'Since then', he says, he has had cause to be reminded that love is a bitter experience, and it is always this scene that epitomises that for him. In Byron's case we know that the details of the poem are somewhat elusive and constrained by his need to be discreet. He had to be careful in case people knew who he was writing about, and in the society he lived in, reputation was very important so he didn't want everyone to know about the affair. Still, he wrote the poem and we can assume that the woman it is addressed to read it.

Overall I think both poets show a remarkable degree of self-absorbed arrogance in how they present their feelings about the end of a relationship. Both feel to some degree wronged and they come across as a rather self-pitying. I do wonder what the women in question would have said in reply to these poems. Byron is the angrier of the two, but both are bitter and both have been changed by their experience of love that failed.

> Exploration of ideas/perspectives/contextual factors shown by specific, detailed links between context/text/task.

> Good use of embedded quotation.

> Convincing and critical analysis and exploration.

> Exploration of ideas/perspectives/contextual factors shown by specific, detailed links between context/text/task.

> Clear personal response is given.

> Clear conclusion that refers back to the question.

Marks Scheme

For the anthology question, your answer will be assessed on three Assessment Objectives (AOs). AO1 and AO2 are each worth up to 12 marks and AO3 is worth up to 6 marks.

- AO1 - Critical, exploratory comparison; judicious use of precise references to support interpretations.
- AO2 - Analysis of writers' methods with subject terminology used judiciously; exploration of effects of writer's methods on reader.
- AO3 - Exploration of ideas/perspectives/contextual factors shown by specific, detailed links between context/text/task.

Examiner's Comment

- This is a Level 5 response. It is a strong answer which focuses on detail in an analytical manner and makes very clear links between the poems.
- The answer is focused and demonstrates clear understanding of both poems. The comparison clearly explains the effect of writers' methods in language, structure and form.
- This student uses subject terminology appropriately to support the points made. Different interpretations are explored, including reference to contextual aspects, clearly related to the texts and the specific question asked.

> **Key Point**
>
> The mark scheme descriptions are available on the AQA website and are worth reading to give you an idea of what the examiner will be looking for.

Mixed Exam-Style Questions

Note: In the exam, each question will only refer to one poem. You will need to choose the other poem. For the purposes of these exam-style questions, a poem has been suggested (in brackets) to make the comparison with. This is shown in the answer section at the back of the book.

1 *When We Two Parted* (Compare with *The Farmer's Bride*)
Compare how poets present ideas about a failed relationship in 'When We Two Parted' and in **one** other poem from 'Love and Relationships'.
Continue your answer on a separate piece of paper.

30 marks

2 *Love's Philosophy* (Compare with *Sonnet 29*)
Compare how poets use nature to present ideas about love in 'Love's Philosophy' and in **one** other poem from 'Love and Relationships'.
Continue your answer on a separate piece of paper.

30 marks

3   *Porphyria's Lover* (Compare with *Singh Song!*)

Compare how poets use voice to present a relationship in 'Porphyria's Lover' and in **one** other poem from 'Love and Relationships'.

Continue your answer on a separate piece of paper.

30 marks

4   *Walking Away* (Compare with *Eden Rock*)

Compare how poets present ideas about love between parent and child in 'Walking Away' and in **one** other poem from 'Love and Relationships'.

Continue your answer on a separate piece of paper.

30 marks

5 *Winter Swans* (Compare with *Neutral Tones*)
Compare how poets use a natural setting to present a relationship in 'Winter Swans' and in **one** other poem from 'Love and Relationships'.
Continue your answer on a separate piece of paper.

30 marks

6 *Climbing My Grandfather* (Compare with *Follower*)
Compare how poets present a child's perspective of a relationship in 'Climbing My Grandfather' and in **one** other poem from 'Love and Relationships'.
Continue your answer on a separate piece of paper.

30 marks

7 ***Mother, any distance*** (Compare with ***Before You Were Mine***)

Compare how poets present attitudes towards a parent in 'Mother, any distance' and in **one** other poem from 'Love and Relationships'.

Continue your answer on a separate piece of paper.

30 marks

8 ***Letters from Yorkshire*** (Compare with ***Sonnet 29***)

Compare how poets present ideas about separation in relationships in 'Letters from Yorkshire' and in **one** other poem from 'Love and Relationships'.

Continue your answer on a separate piece of paper.

30 marks

Mixed Exam-Style Questions

9 **The Farmer's Bride** (Compare with *Porphyria's Lover*)

Compare how poets present attitudes towards women in 'The Farmer's Bride' and in **one** other poem from 'Love and Relationships'.

Continue your answer on a separate piece of paper.

30 marks

10 **Sonnet 29** (Compare with *Letters from Yorkshire*)

Compare how poets present attitudes towards romantic love in 'Sonnet 29' and in **one** other poem from 'Love and Relationships'.

Continue your answer on a separate piece of paper.

30 marks

11 *Singh Song!* (Compare with *The Farmer's Bride*)

Compare how poets present ideas about marriage in 'Singh Song!' and in **one** other poem from 'Love and Relationships'.

Continue your answer on a separate piece of paper.

30 marks

12 *Eden Rock* (Compare with *Before You Were Mine*)

Compare how poets present ideas about the love of a child for a parent in 'Eden Rock' and in **one** other poem from 'Love and Relationships'.

Continue your answer on a separate piece of paper.

30 marks

13 *Neutral Tones* (Compare with *Eden Rock*)

Compare how poets use memory to present the experience of love in 'Neutral Tones' and in **one** other poem from 'Love and Relationships'.

Continue your answer on a separate piece of paper.

30 marks

14 *Follower* (Compare with *Walking Away*)

Compare how poets present ideas about how time changes relationships in 'Follower' and in **one** other poem from 'Love and Relationships'.

Continue your answer on a separate piece of paper.

30 marks

15 **Before You Were Mine** (Compare with **Mother, any distance**)

Compare how poets present ideas about the complexities of parental love in 'Before You Were Mine' and in **one** other poem from 'Love and Relationships'.

Continue your answer on a separate piece of paper.

30 marks

Answers

Page 9 Quick Test answers
1. A few years ago.
2. No
3. The other person.

Page 11 Quick Test Answers
1. With examples of connected things in nature.
2. To persuade someone to return his love.
3. With a rhetorical question.

Page 14 Quick Test Answers
1. Stormy.
2. He strangled her with her own hair.
3. Porphyria is a rare blood disorder that may cause mental, nervous or skin problems.

Page 17 Quick Test Answers
1. A sonnet
2. Four
3. Her lover (Robert Browning)

When We Two Parted

1. A
2. She forgot him; she deceived him.
3. Any three of: cold, name, long, silence, tears, they/thee
4. ABABCDCD
5. That his feelings about their relationship are the same now as they were when it ended.
6. pale, cold, chill; They suggest the relationship is over; It has no colour and no life.
7. He uses tenses – past tense and present tense.
8. a) vows, broken, light, fame, hear, name, share, shame. b) They are the important words in the lines.
9. bitterness
10. shudder

Love's Philosophy

1. To add force to his argument with a direct appeal.
2. Three of: fountains, rivers, oceans, winds.
3. 'kiss' and 'clasp'
4. He brings in the sun (sunshine) and moon (moonbeams).
5. He means God's law, as shown through nature. By claiming that not to do as nature does would be to break God's law.
6. It adds force to his argument and suggests he is building up to a climax.
7. All the examples from nature are linked together syntactically and come to a full stop in verse 1 and a colon in verse 2, which gives the sense of a dramatic pause before the rhetorical question each time.
8. assertive

9. It personifies nature, attributing human emotions to natural things. It is an example of the pathetic fallacy.
10. You could argue either way. It is a very controlled and forceful argument, but whether you would be convinced might depend on how Romantic you are!

Porphyria's Lover

1. He describes the weather (stormy) and that it is night time. Everything in nature outside the cottage speaks of disturbance and bad-humour, reflecting the speaker's state of mind, inside the cottage.
2. She transforms it, bringing light and warmth.
3. She lets her hair fall, puts her arm around his waist and puts his cheek on her shoulder.
4. It tells us that he is depressed and miserable – heart-broken, though we don't know why.
5. Lines 36–7 'I found/A thing to do'.
6. He wants to possess her entirely and for ever. He thinks this is what she wanted, also.
7. It is very controlled, methodical and tightly structured with a regular rhyme scheme and mostly regular rhythm. Several lines upset the rhythm, showing the speaker's disturbed state of mind.
8. A flower (52); a doll

9. He loves Porphyria so much that he wants to possess her for ever. He 'achieves' this by murdering her.
10. He wants to suggest that God approves of his actions; he wants readers to question whether God exists.

Sonnet 29 – 'I think of thee!'

1. A vine that winds itself around a tree.
2. As a vine wraps around a tree, her thoughts wrap around her lover.
3. A palm tree.
4. The vine is the speaker's thoughts (female poet; Elizabeth Barrett Browning) and the tree is her lover (a man; Robert Browning).
5. An extended metaphor.
6. It repeats the phrase 'I think of thee', but changes it to the negative 'I do not think of thee'.
7. She means that when she is near her lover she is so joyful to be in his presence that she doesn't need to have thoughts of him at all.
8. Encircle or surround
9. When she is near her lover she feels free.
10. It has 14 lines; it has a clear rhyme pattern.

Page 23 Quick Test Answers
1. From: desolate, bleak, despair, hopeless, negative

2. 'Neutral' describes the lack of colour and excitement. 'Tones' refers to the colour and mood.
3. The tight structure reflects the poet's constricted emotions.

Page 25 Quick Test Answers
1. Any three of: a winter's day, a frightened fay, a hare, a mouse, a leveret, a young larch tree, wild violets.
2. In the second verse the farmer says, 'We chased her' and 'We caught her'.
3. The farmer understands and admires nature, but his wife's response to her fear of men is to draw closer to animals and to distance herself from him.

Page 27 Quick Test Answers
1. A father.
2. Watching his son leave a football game and walk away from him back to school.
3. The son.

Page 29 Quick Test Answers
1. Winter.
2. She is a writer of some kind.
3. He plants, digs and sows outdoors, so he may be a farmer or a gardener.

Neutral Tones

1. Uses commas to create short phrases. Makes the lines choppy and jerky — as if argumentative and bad-tempered.
2. white, gray, grayish
3. They tell us that this happened some time ago.
4. 'And' shows the poet linking, sequencing and accumulating all the various elements of the poem. It builds and layers the elements that create the mood of the poem.
5. 'God-curst sun'.
6. 'alive enough to have strength to die'.
7. The words we spoke to each other served only make our love even less.
8. C
9. It brings the poem full circle, which is satisfying to the reader. It also shows there has been no forward movement between them. They are stuck in the same place, literally and emotionally.

The Farmer's Bride

1. A farmer.
2. Three years.
3. The farmer and other men chased her and brought her home.
4. The farmer keeps her locked in.
5. She sees them as dangerous and harmful.
6. Probably not: the farmer calls her a 'maid' in line 43, so this indicates she is still a virgin. She's also called a 'bride' in the title. They now sleep apart.

7. They make the speaker sound light-hearted and matter-of-fact and this apparent lack of deep emotion indicates that the speaker doesn't really understand what has happened to his wife, and their relationship. It makes him sound simple: almost childish.

8. 1) It indicates the rural setting of the poem – the farmer and his wife live in an isolated, natural landscape. 2) The farmer's appreciation of nature is shown by the similes he uses in the fifth verse.

9. Line 2

10. 'I chose a maid' (1)

Walking Away

1. B
2. 'like a satellite/ Wrenched from its orbit' (4-5); 'Like a winged seed loosened from its parent stem' (12).
3. 18 years ago
4. Because it involved his own young son; because it continues to bother him that he hasn't been able to express his complex feelings about the parting.
5. It emphasises the main theme of the poem – separation.
6. That in order to grow up, children have to separate from their parents; that their parents have to let them go and in doing so they show their love.
7. He is struggling to convey (express) his own thoughts and feelings.
8. 'proved' may mean 'shown to be real or true'. It could mean that love that allows freedom is genuine love.

Letters from Yorkshire

1. Spends a lot of time outdoors.
2. He wants to tell her what is happening in the natural world, in Yorkshire. It is his 'news'.
3. She may be a journalist or a writer. 'Headlines' suggests she's a news writer, perhaps.
4. No. The speaker says, 'It's not romance, simply how things are.' They may be close friends, or blood relatives.
5. By letter; also by unspoken 'messages' between them.
6. It suggests that they are very close – they can communicate without words.
7. It is cold and the work is hard. He breaks ice; clears snow.
8. He — outdoors, hard physical labour, immersed in the natural world, such as the arrival of lapwings is news; She — indoors, works with words, writes 'headlines'.
9. He writes letters to her of what is happening in Yorkshire. She writes words on a screen. She values his letters because they bring 'air and light' to her indoor existence. By contrast, her screen is 'blank'.
10. She questions the validity of her own lifestyle, compared to his. He is in close daily contact with the natural world, whereas she is not.

When We Two Parted

1. The poet himself.
2. B
3. two
4. several years
5. a) The poet repeats the phrase 'silence and tears'. b) It shows that the end of the relationship several years before continues to cause him pain now.
6. That the other person's reputation (in society) is not as good as it once was: there has been a scandal of some sort.
7. The affair was conducted in secret ('in secret we met' (25), so he must keep it that way.
8. He could mean that only one of them was broken-hearted — he was, but she wasn't. It could mean that the end of the relationship was not important enough to break their hearts wholly.
9. Himself

Love's Philosophy

1. Three from: mountains, waves, flowers, sunlight, moonbeams.
2. Each verse uses the same rhyme scheme and each has 8 lines; in each verse the poet creates a list of things in the natural world that are connected to each other and finishes with a rhetorical question.
3. Mingle, mix and meet.
4. With a rhetorical question.
5. It refers to Shelley's thoughts about seeking to understand love.
6. playful
7. He wants to appeal to the other person's reason — but his case is to plead for her love. The 'facts' he presents her with are really his interpretations of natural events.
8. It places the onus on the other person to be active, not passive.
9. He creates lists of examples of nature's connectedness and uses personification to illustrate his argument that everything in the universe is in love.
10. Pathetic fallacy.

Porphyria's Lover

1. She makes a fire, bringing warmth and light. She invites his attention by letting down her hair, embracing him, and placing his cheek on her shoulder.
2. It connects his actions together as if they are a logical and ordinary course of action; it indicates his obsessive state of mind.
3. The poem is tightly structured, with a regular rhyme scheme and mostly regular rhythm. Several lines upset the rhythm, showing the speaker's disturbed state of mind. It shows that the speaker thinks there is nothing unusual or odd about what the events he describes.
4. It suggests his thought processes are fragmented.

5. There is a suggestion that she had been at a party ('gay feast', line 27).
6. He wants to lessen the impact of his crime. He wants the reader to understand that he thinks the act was an act of love, not violence.
7. 'And give herself to me for ever' (25); 'That moment she was mine, mine' (36).
8. Dramatic monologue.
9. It is what Porphyria herself wanted also, but was too weak to do so.
10. They sit together, but this time Porphyria's dead cheek is on his shoulder.

Sonnet 29 – 'I think of thee!'

1. Each marks a change of direction or turning point in the speaker's train of thought.
2. B
3. a) wild vines represent the speaker's passionate thoughts (female poet; Elizabeth Barrett Browning) b) the tree is her lover (a man; Robert Browning).
4. Yes. She starts by describing how her thoughts, like vines covering a tree, cover her lover's presence when they are apart. Then she imagines how by coming closer to her, and being in her presence, her lover can break through those thoughts (vines) and finishes by saying that when she is in her lover's presence, she doesn't need to have thoughts of him anyway — to be near him, in his shadow, is freedom.
5. ABBA ABBA CBCBCB. It divides the poem up into two quatrains and a sestet.
6. A group of six lines.
7. To emphasise that 'thee' is the object of the speaker's passionate love.
8. That the speaker would much rather have her lover near her in person than only her thoughts of him, when they are apart.
9. 'deep joy' (12)
10. To emphasise the depth and strength of her feelings.

Page 39 Quick Test Answers
1. It suggests the 'Garden of Eden' in the Bible, the original and perfect natural home of Adam and Eve.
2. Three: the speaker as a child, his mother and his father.
3. The final line: 'I had not thought that it would be like this.'

Page 41 Quick Test Answers
1. A field being ploughed.
2. The poet as a child and his father, and the poet now and his father.
3. Be a farmer, like his father.

Page 43 Quick Test Answers
1. A son.
2. His mother.
3. He reaches through a skylight towards the sky.

Page 45 Quick Test Answers
1. The speaker's mother.
2. A daughter.
3. The late 1940s and 1950s.

Eden Rock

1. B
2. From: H.P. sauce, thermos bottle, plates and tin cups.
3. His father's suit; his mother's dress; her hat (and ribbon); the colour of her hair.
4. It tells us the poet, now older, is looking back on an event in the past.
5. a) otherworldliness and
   b) death.
6. The age of his parents; the word 'same'; the use of the present continuous tense.
7. Use of 'I' (18)
8. ABAB
9. 'Slowly' and 'Leisurely'.
10. Present tense. Creates a sense of immediacy.

Follower

1. C
2. 'set the wing'; 'fit the bright steel-pointed sock'; 'At the headrig'.
3. 'like a full sail strung'; 'hob-nailed wake'; 'polished sod'.
4. It indicates the differences between 'then' and 'now'.
5. globed; strained; sweating.
6. He uses the past tense; he talks about growing up; he uses the word 'today'.
7. He literally followed his father around the farm; he metaphorically followed his father in admiring him and wanting to be a farmer when he grew up.
8. ABAB
9. In the second verse, the consonance of the /ck/, /p/ and /t/ sounds.
10. The word contrasts the father's movement, now he is old, with the description of his physical majesty of movement and skill as a young farmer, in the first four verses. It also links the young poet's movements, 'tripping' and 'falling' when he was young, with his father's movements now.

Mother, any distance

1. A son and his mother take measurements of his new house for furnishing and decoration.
2. Extended metaphor.
3. He is likening himself to an explorer, linked to his 'base' – his mother. The images suggest he is both excited and nervous about leaving his mother's home.
4. 'acres' and 'prairies'. It suggests the house is large and completely empty.
5. Anchor is his mother. Kite is the speaker.
6. The space between them grows bigger as the son moves further up the house. They remain connected by a measuring tape that grows tauter and tauter.
7. '... your fingertips still pinch /the last one-hundredth of an inch'
8. It suggests he still feels unsure about whether he can take this step towards independence. He doesn't know if he

will succeed (fly) or fail (fall).
9. It is a loose sonnet form, with 15 lines instead of the usual 14 and with a rhyme scheme that begins formally and then disintegrates into free verse. It mirrors the speaker's moving away from the formality of home and parents, to freedom and independence. [2]
10. It may suggest that the speaker will always on some level, need his mother to be there, no matter what the literal distance between them.

Before You Were Mine

1. polka-dot dress; the reference to Marilyn Monroe in a famous photograph from the 1950s.
2. 10
3. Playing with her mother's red shoes; her mother teaching her dance steps.
4. Ten years.
5. It emphasises the speaker's feeling of possessing of her mother.
6. It speaks of the daughter possessing the mother; traditionally it is the other way around.
7. 'in the ballroom with the thousand eyes, the fizzy, movie tomorrows'.
8. It suggests that her mother's life took a wrong turn; that she might have expected a different life to the one she had. The star pavement links back to the reference to glitzy films and Marilyn Monroe – the Hollywood Walk of Fame.
9. The speaker (daughter) speaks the questions to her mother, in a role reversal. The irony is that these are questions that a mother might ask of her daughter.
10. That the relationship endures and that they will always be connected through the speaker's memories of her mother's glamorous life before she was born.

Neutral Tones

1. D. All the above are present in the poem.
2. By a pond.
3. Late autumn or winter
4. They probably argue and blame each other for the failed relationship.
5. Her eyes seem to recall things that happened in the past, perhaps when their love was young and new, but which are boring now.
6. strength
7. bleak
8. Even God is displeased with this situation – so much so that he drains all life and colour from the sun.
9. The words 'Since then'; the use of the past tense.
10. 'wrings with wrong' is an example of alliteration. The repeated 'r' sounds make us feel the poet's pain and bitterness.

The Farmer's Bride

1. The use of exclamations 'Oh! my God' (44) and questions 'But what to me?' (33) give the poem a colloquial tone.
2. Yes, they are mismatched. 1) she ran away months after marrying ('runned away' (9)) 2) she does not speak (29) 3) they sleep apart (42).
3. Three from: bide and woo (3); 'twasn't (7); 'mong (10), fay (8), her be (10); abed (11); fetched (18).
4. 'But what to me? (33).
5. Monologue.
6. confused
7. Women are seen as commodities to be given and taken in marriage, and held under lock and key when they show signs of independence.
8. They indicate her isolation.
9. 'Out 'mong the sheep' (10); 'Not near, not near!' (25). The direct speech adds dramatic impact and immediacy. Line 25 emphasises that the wife is dumb, as she speaks with her eyes, not her voice.
10. The repetition and rhyme give a very lyrical and rich sound to the lines, almost sing-song. They are different to the rest of the poem because of the emotion they contain. The farmer suddenly cannot contain his feelings, which have been suppressed in the rest of the poem.

Walking Away

1. At a school football pitch in early autumn.
2. It encapsulates the theme of separation in the poem.
3. The description of the autumn day 'with leaves just turning'.
4. That the son (the satellite) is moving away from close parental protection (the orbit). It implies that the son and father were very close, but now the relationship is changing.
5. a) It suggests the son cannot yet 'fly' by himself, like a chick that is not quite ready to leave the nest. b) It suggests that the father still feels protective and that his son is not quite ready to move away from the father's protection.
6. B and C
7. The word suggests ongoing, nagging pain. (It brings to mind rodents (rats or mice) gnawing in a determined way, and the image is unpleasant.) The effect is to help us understand that the memory has been troubling the poet for a long time.
8. 'Perhaps' and 'roughly' (7).

Letters from Yorkshire

1. News of the changing seasons, such as the arrival of the first lapwings.
2. He may not have access to the internet or a mobile phone. The poem was written in the early 2000s when mobile phones were not so widely available. His rural lifestyle means that he might not have cause to

need one either.
Or he could belong to an older generation which feels more comfortable writing letters.
3. The pronouns shift from third to second person to make the other person seem closer to the speaker.
4. Very important. They bring 'air and light' which are absent from her lifestyle.
5. His outdoor lifestyle in Yorkshire.
6. Possibly. She talks of the 'blank screen' and how his letters bring 'air and light' to her world. She also asks the question 'Is your life more real …?' as if comparing the two.
7. That they are very close and share the same thoughts and feelings about each other.
8. It gives the sense that this situation and relationship is ongoing.
9. When they say, 'You wouldn't say so'.
10. The poet juxtaposes their contrasting lifestyles, yet shows how, through letters, words and unspoken messages between their 'souls', they remain in close contact.

Page 55 Quick Test Answers
1. By a lake.
2. winter
3. swans

Page 58 Quick Test Answers
1. He uses contrasting images of comfort and threat to describe her.
2. It helps create an intimate, romantic tone which reflects the content of the section where the young couple dream together.
3. Singh is a name traditionally given to all Sikh boys and the title also reflects the shopkeeper's melodic accent and intonation. The pun reflects the light humour that is present throughout the poem.
4. It creates the feeling that there are a large number of people speaking to him this way, and that it is a regular occurrence.

Page 61 Quick Test Answers
1. A small child climbs up his grandfather's body.
2. A small child.
3. His grandfather's beating heart.

Winter Swans

1. Monogamy (having only one partner in their whole life).
2. There has been a storm.
3. The earth is sodden with water and 'gulps' for breath as if it is drowning, like the relationship, which is in trouble.
4. They move in unison; they are able to right themselves after going under.
5. 'stilling water'
6. iceberg; porcelain.

7. Perhaps he wants the significance of the statement to hang in the air between them; perhaps his 'reply' is to hold his partner's hand.
8. Calm and peaceful. 'slow-stepping' and the image of the hands swimming together like wings indicate this.
9. That the couple are holding hands.
10. The image of their held hands being like a pair of wings folding together after flight.

Singh Song!

1. The name 'Singh' sounds like 'sing'. Sing-song means to speak in rising and falling tones, like a children's chant or song.
2. That he is not a native English speaker.
3. It is a dramatic monologue.
4. It suggests that she is in control; in the position of power.
5. They are dreaming of a different life, suggesting they are unhappy with their current existence.
6. It is a continual reminder of the reality of life for the speaker.
7. Two from: red crew cut, Tartan sari, making fun of his father; donkey jacket; swearing at his mother.
8. She eats traditional Indian food; she wears a sari.
9. It shows that the speaker is proud of and possessive of his wife.
10. Because the speaker works in a shop; it makes fun of stereotypes about Indian shopkeepers.

Climbing My Grandfather

1. A mountain.
2. To climb free, without a safety net or rope.
3. Parts of the mountain that he has to climb.
4. He feels a bit nervous at times ('for climbing has its dangers') but at other times the mountain offers him rest and refreshment; The same with his grandfather, who is an imposing figure and whom he respects, but who also loves him and who is benevolent.
5. There are several: age, size and solidity are obvious ones.
6. 'place my feet/gently in the old stitches and move on' (11-12).
7. It is split into sentences that divide the sequence of the climb into stages as the child goes from foot to summit.
8. Tired, but elated, and sure of his grandfather's love.
9. He is giving his grandfather a kiss.
10. The monosyllables give the line a beat like the beating of a heart.

Eden Rock

1. Three: the poet, his father and his mother.
2. D. The vivid and exact details suggest it was a real event that happened in the speaker's past, so a memory, but the vagueness of the location and the

unnaturalness of the images 'whitening sky' and 'three suns', together with the final line which makes it clear that the speaker is looking back on the past, prompt us to re-evaluate the first three verses as perhaps being a description of a dream.
3. For example, the 'whitening sky'; 'three suns', create a sense of mystery and unease.
4. Direct speech — gives immediacy to the poem and adds the idea of feeling surprised at remembering seemingly small incidents.
5. To create a detailed picture of the scene — like a photograph.
6. (a) love (b) separated
7. mysterious
8. He is excited.
9. It creates a sense of immediacy: the past is made present and real to the reader.
10. It tells us the poet is older now. Perhaps he is disappointed by his life when he remembers how happy his parents once were.

Follower

1. It describes how the poet feels about his father. He literally followed him as a child and he admired his father so much he wanted to follow in his footsteps and become a farmer when he grew up.
2. 'His shoulders globed like a full sail strung/Between the shafts and the furrow.'
3. The poet is older now as he writes the poem and his father is an old man; The horses used to plough the fields show it happened at a time before mechanisation.
4. B
5. He uses a considerable number of details and technical words in the poem.
6. A, D
7. 'angled', 'mapping' and 'exactly'.
8. Line 17: 'I wanted to grow up and plough'.
9. 'But' (21).
10. Yes: 'and will not go away' shows some annoyance at his father; but it is also affectionate.

Mother, any distance

1. A
2. The sonnet.
3. Yes, in that the speaker describes through metaphor his strong feelings for his mother, which are mixed with feeling daunted and nervous about moving away from her.
4. The image of the tape measure 'line' reeling out years suggests the history they share.
5. It suggests the difference in age between the two generations and also that the further away he goes from his mother, the closer he feels.
6. A measuring tape.

7. It links back to the space imagery used earlier in the poem and has another meaning as a verb, 'to emerge from an egg' so like a fledgling the speaker is about to take flight on his own.
8. 'base'; 'Anchor'
9. the 'endless sky'; his independence/ freedom.
10. The image of the speaker as a kite in line 8.

Before You Were Mine

1. She makes references to herself as 'ten years away' and 'I'm not here yet'; though not yet born, she includes herself in her mother's life.
2. The ghost of her mother (in her previous life before the speaker was born).
3. Her mother's mother ('Ma').
4. They conjure up a romanticised and exciting image of her mother's previous existence.
5. A mirror ball that reflects the light; the fact that her mother attracted a lot of attention from people/she was popular.
6. 'stamping stars from the wrong pavement.' (The word 'wrong' suggests that the mother ended up in the wrong place.)
7. It is both **nostalgic** for and **wistful**; about the mother's previous life. The speaker has complex feelings about the life her mother led before she was born. She is both envious and admiring.
8. It suggests that her mother's life changed for ever once she had a baby and that she herself would reminisce about her previous life, to her daughter.
9. Glasgow
10. It gives a sense of immediacy, even though she is describing the imagined past.

Winter Swans

1. Swans on a lake.
2. 'waterlogged'; 'gulping for breath'.
3. Monogamy 'they mate for life' and faithfulness.
4. 'silent and apart'.
5. They make a 'show' of tipping their heads downwards in unison (together).
6. 'like boats righting in rough weather'.
7. To go around the edge; to avoid an issue. The couple literally go around the edge of the lake; they may be avoiding talking about an issue which has caused a rift between them.
8. It may suggest that though this might be a start at renewal of the relationship, the future is still uncertain.
9. They are moving together in unison, like the swans moved; they are no longer apart.
10. Like the swans, they have 'swum' together; and they are 'like a pair of wings settling after flight'.

Singh Song!

1. He runs his father's shop.
2. He is both frightened by her ('eyes ov a gun') and thinks she's cuddly and cute ('tummy ov a teddy').
3. It has a chorus, rhyme and repeated phrases and lines.
4. The title, 'Singh Song!' and 'brightey moon'.
5. comical
6. In a precinct, in the 'Indian road'.
7. He shuts up the shop when it's quiet to have sex with her; he finds her unconventionality attractive; he enjoys the ways she rebels against tradition.
8. The pun in the title suggests that the poem is playful and humorous in tone.
9. That the speaker is poking fun at his customers through his wife's questions.
10. He doesn't much care what they think. He never replies to their complaints.

Climbing My Grandfather

1. It is divided into sentences that match the stages of the child's climb; it is one long verse with a regular line length to echo the rhythm of the climb.
2. The dusty, cracked brogues, earth-stained hands and splintered nails (suggest he had a physical job outside) His scar suggest he has perhaps been injured or wounded.
3. 'warm ice'; 'smiling mouth'.
4. He says 'for climbing has its dangers' so we might think so, but it may be that this is a humorous reference since the whole poem is 'mock heroic'.
5. He sees clouds and birds circle. Humorous to him because his grandfather's head seems as high as a mountain summit.
6. Because high mountains are icy near the summit. Warm because his grandfather is a 'human mountain'.
7. He feels bold; also he knows his grandfather won't let him fall.
8. It gives the narrative a sense of immediacy and pace as the child completes the climb bit by bit.
9. First (2); by (5); at (13); then (3).
10. 'warm ice'; 'overhanging shirt'; 'glassy ridge of a scar'; 'earth-stained hand'; 'brogues, dusty and cracked'; 'hair (soft and white at this altitude)'. (Any two).

1. When We Two Parted/The Farmer's Bride

Suggested content:

- Consider the speakers' feelings: Byron's is bitter, knowing, but resigned; Mew's is poignant and hurt, doesn't quite understand what his wife wants.
- Both speakers are hurt by the failure of the relationship, but react in different ways: Byron's speaker wants to protect himself against damage to his reputation; Mew's is also aware of society's pressures

and is sad, but also resentful of his wife's lack of feeling for him.
- Compare the use and effects of rhythm: Byron's strict and formal two-beat rhythm drives the poem along, relentlessly, suggesting anger beneath the surface. Mew's four beats are gentler and more sing-song and bely the tragic content.
- Consider the use and effect of imagery: Mew uses natural imagery as befits the rural setting to show that the wife is part of nature, untamed by society. Byron uses parts of the body (brow, kiss, ear, heart) to refer to aspects of their relationship which has splintered into bits.
- Contrast the voice and perspective – control (Byron) vs. vulnerability (Mew) and the tone. Byron's is a personal address, using the first and second person. Mew's speaker uses the more impersonal third person to refer to his wife, emphasising the distance between them.
- Consider the differing contexts of the poems. Byron's has personal resonance for the poet, yet he chose to make his personal life public in writing the poem, while Mew was adopting a persona, choosing to highlight a social problem of arranged rural marriage, via the dramatic monologue.

2. Love's Philosophy/Sonnet 29

Suggested content:

- Show how both poets use natural imagery to convey aspects of love. Both make the strong use of personal voice 'I' and 'thee', first-person to make their pleas more direct. Both address their lover directly.
- Poet's methods: Shelley uses formal structure (strict rhyme and rhythm) to mount two persuasive arguments, one in each verse. Each mirrors the other to some degree; each ends with a question; the effect is logical, perhaps cold. Barrett Browning also uses formal structure of a love sonnet (three quatrains and a couplet) to present a developing train of thought. The use of punctuation, broken with dashes, exclamations and use of enjambment conveys a breathless passion.
- Barrett Browning uses one central image of her love as a vine wrapping around a palm-tree (her lover) – it is a strongly personal image. Shelley's natural imagery is less personal and more varied, but presents all of nature as embracing lovers to further his persuasive plea.
- Both poets are writing in the Romantic tradition, using nature to symbolise aspects of human love, Shelley uses pathetic fallacy, i.e. endowing nature with human attributes. Compare to how Barrett Browning endows herself and her lover with the natural attributes of a vine and palm tree.

3. Porphyria's Lover/Singh Song!

Suggested content:

- Both poets adopt a persona and use the dramatic monologue form to present a relationship.
- Both speakers challenge stereotypes. Browning's speaker plays with conventions of the Victorian woman as 'angel' in describing Porphyria's blond hair, blue eyes and domesticity, adoration of her lover, but then he murders her to 'consummate' their union. Nagra's speaker enjoys his wife's unconventionality as an Indian wife – her Tartan sari, red crew cut and the way she challenges his parents' authority.
- Dramatic monologue form means that we only learn about the other person in the relationship through the speaker. The reader must read between the lines as there is a gap between what the speaker says and what is revealed.
- In Browning's poem we gradually learn more about the speaker's state of mind and the reader guesses at the history of their relationship through clues he gives (for example we guess that Porphyria comes from a different class and that they would never be allowed to marry; they meet in secret). In *Singh Song!* we gather that the marriage has been arranged, but that the speaker has strong sexual attraction for his wife.
- Both speakers present sexual encounters, but in Browning's poem it is suggested according to the conventions of romantic poetry and the context in which the poem was written ('give herself for me for ever'), while in Nagra's poem it is explicit ('made luv/like vee rowing through Putney').
- Both speakers use a formal structure and rhyme scheme. In Browning's poem the effect is to indicate the speaker's conventionality and rationality – it helps to persuade readers that the relationship he describes is perfectly normal. In Nagra's poem, the structure, with its repeated refrains, reminds us of a child's song or a playground rhyme, giving a tone of playfulness and humour which is appropriate for the relationship of a young married couple.

4. Walking Away/Eden Rock

Suggested content:

- Both poems are presented as poignant memories of a particular event. Causley remembers a picnic with his parents. Day Lewis remembers his son after a football match walking away from him back towards school.
- Both poems express nostalgia about the past event, but Causley presents the event as a snapshot using the third person and present tense, and we don't realise it is a memory until the poignant final line of the poem.

Day Lewis introduces the poem as a memory in the first line – 'eighteen years ago' and addresses his son directly.

- Causley presents us with a sense of mystery and other-worldliness when he says 'The sky whitens as if lit by three suns' and we sense that his love for his parents has a mystical element. Later in the poem we realise this is because they are dead. The symbolism of crossing the stream-path indicates that perhaps he will rejoin his parents at some point, when he dies.
- Day Lewis on the other hand presents parental love as a painful, but necessary, letting go, with images that suggest his son leaving the parental 'orbit' and finding his independence; a 'half-fledged thing' that his father's instinct is to protect, but that he realises he must allow to go free. Day Lewis mentions God's sacrifice of his Son to give meaning to his thoughts.
- Both poems use interrupted syntax and detailed imagery to evoke the very strong emotional bonds between parent and child. Causley's the child for the parents and Day Lewis the parent for the child. Both in different ways show the struggle to control their feelings in expressing the exquisite, but necessary pain of separation.

5. Winter Swans/Neutral Tones

Suggested content:

- Both poems describe a memory of an event that took place in a natural setting. Hardy's poem describes a dead, static relationship that is reflected in the colourless and lifeless winter scene of trees and a pond with dead leaves strewed around. Shears presents an encounter with swans that gives hope that a rift in a relationship can be healed.
- Both poems are written in the first-person, addressing the 'you' – the other person in the relationship. Hardy's was written to his wife who had died at the time he wrote the poem. The relationship was definitely over, though the memory of it still had the power to hurt him. By contrast, Shears poem is more quietly optimistic that this relationship could be healed. The final line is unfinished and the poem ends in a couplet with no punctuation, giving us the sense that the relationship is ongoing.
- In Shears' poem, the couple interact with and interpret what they observe of the swans' behaviour. The swans model unity and monogamy in their relationship. The couple take a positive message from this for their own relationship, so that their hands swim towards each other and they move 'slow-stepping' together after the swans have left. By contrast, nature in Hardy's poem is motionless, reflecting the dreary and dead quality of

the relationship, and offers no hope or respite. Hardy likens his wife's 'grin of bitterness' to a bird, but it is 'ominous', compared to the swans in Shears which offer the couple first a distraction from their own discord and then a lesson in harmony and peace.

- Both poets use striking images of a wintry scene to suggest aspects of the relationships. Shears has 'waterlogged earth gulping for breath', suggesting a relationship that is struggling to stay alive and Hardy has 'grayish leaves', an 'ominous bird' and a 'God-curst sun' as fitting emblems of a love that is completely over and dead.

6. Climbing My Grandfather/Follower

Suggested content:

- Both poets present a child's relationship with an older relative. In Heaney's poem it is with his father, while in Waterhouse's it is with his grandfather. Both use a child's perspective to convey the child's respect for the power, age and stability of the relative.
- For Waterhouse, this is shown using an extended metaphor of his grandfather as a mountain that the child climbs, stage by stage. Heaney also uses a metaphor of a ship to indicate his father's majesty and stateliness as he ploughs a field using horses – a highly skilled task.
- In both poems the child is young, but Waterhouse's speaker is the younger barely a toddler so his grandfather seems absolutely huge to the child. The grandfather's body and clothing are described as geological features – his shirt is an overhang; his scar a ridge, etc. Heaney's speaker is older, but recalls the small child who followed in his father's wake as he ploughed and sometimes rode on his back. The young Heaney is full of admiration for his father's expertise. The words 'An expert.' are given prominence at the start of a line. He also indicates his father's strength and power 'broad shadow', just as Waterhouse does in 'firm shoulder' for his grandfather.
- Waterhouse indicates that his grandfather led an outdoor life and worked a physical job ('earth-stained hands and dusty brogues'), as did Heaney's father. Both poets convey a sense that the older relative belongs to a different generation in their clothing and by trade, and both give a sense of the older relative possessing a calm assurance – in the way the grandfather tolerates and helps the toddler to climb him, and in the way that the father tolerated the 'Yapping' of the young 'nuisance' Heaney.
- For Heaney, the memory of his father contrasts with their current situation where his father now follows him, the son. Now the father 'stumbling/Behind me' is a nuisance, so the roles have

been reversed. Heaney breaks with the child's perspective to add this coda to the poem, while Waterhouse retains the child's perspective throughout.

- Heaney's use of controlled rhyme, rhythm and quatrains mirrors the controlled expertise of his father's ploughing and is, in its way, a homage to his father's expertise. By contrast, Waterhouse uses long sentences in one long verse, which mark the stages of the child's climb. Both use an adult voice and mature poetic techniques to convey the child's perspective.

7. Mother, any distance/Before You Were Mine

Suggested content:

- Duffy and Armitage both present love poems to their mothers, but in *Before You Were Mine*, Duffy depicts her mother's life before the poet was born, while Armitage describes the situation of his mother helping him to take measurements of his new house. This is a metaphor for how the two of them are moving apart while remaining in contact.
- Both poets refer to the complexities of the parent-child relationship. Duffy's speaker tries to take possession of her mother's life before the poet was born, extending the possession and closeness that the daughter feels for the mother, by part-imagining, and in part drawing on the memories that the mother shared with the daughter. By contrast, Armitage's speaker sees the relationship as one of separation and growing independence for the son, but always retaining a connection, with the mother described as a 'base' and 'Anchor' to his 'Kite'.
- Duffy's speaker wants to get closer to her mother and to own all her memories, connected as she is to them via objects, like the mother's high-heeled shoe that the daughter played with and the dances that her mother taught her as they walked home from Mass. Duffy's own memories, and those of her mother, are cleverly woven together, and there is a sense that the poet is slightly envious of, and very admiring of, her mother's glamorous single life of dancing, movies and romances.
- Armitage by contrast sees his mother in relation to himself and acknowledges that his mother is essential to his independence – without her he could not attempt to be free and his speaker is nervous, and even daunted, at the thought of flying free. The images of space exploration and vast open spaces (prairies, acres) that are risky and dangerous, but exhilarating, underline this feeling.
- Both poets indicate the difference in the generations. Duffy with her references to polka dot dresses, Marilyn Monroe and the glitterball in the dance hall era, strongly evokes the imagined glamour of the late 1940s and early 1950s.

Armitage is more subtle. In his poem, his mother still grips the tape using imperial measurements, whereas he has used metric in his quest to reach for freedom.

8. Letters from Yorkshire/Sonnet 29

Suggested content:

- Both poets are women and talk about being separated from a male partner. In Barrett Browning's case this was her fiancé Robert Browning. In Dooley's case the relationship with the male partner is probably platonic (she explicitly states 'It's not romance, simply how things are') yet the couple are very close emotionally.
- Both women speak to their partners from a distance: Dooley is in another city, probably miles away from Yorkshire, where he lives a lifestyle very different from her own. They communicate by letter, and by unspoken messages, soul to soul, that reach across the miles at night. For Barrett Browning, the distance between them leads to her imagining herself as a vine, closely twined around his 'palm-tree'. There is sexual implication in the image. Barrett Browning fantasises about being very close to her absent lover. For Dooley, the separation is breached by his letters and she makes explicit contrasts between the different worlds they each inhabit.
- Barrett Browning has her thoughts breach the distance and for Dooley 'our souls tap out messages'. In the latter poem the speaker begins by picturing him in Yorkshire, using the third person, underlining the separation between them. This separation is gradually lessened as the poem develops, indicated by the use pronouns: 'he' becomes 'you' and finally in the last verse they are together as 'our'. Only in the final three lines do we have a sense that their relationship is a very close one. Though not 'romantic', they have a very strong mutual understanding.
- Barrett Browning on the other hand, uses 'thee' and 'I' throughout and repeats thee over and over in the poem, as if calling to her lover. Her poem is overtly romantic, passionate and personal, written in a traditional sonnet form that develops a train of thought. In a sense she is acting out what she *wants* to happen: to swap her thoughts that bring her lover closer to her in fantasy only, for his real presence, which would banish all thoughts of him by being actually there.
- The two poems provide an interesting contrast between women's roles in the 19th and 20th centuries. *Sonnet 29* presents a woman waiting, and longing, for her fiancé's return, while *Letters from Yorkshire* shows a woman with an independent life and work ruminating on how a relationship can be both distant and close.

9. The Farmer's Bride /Porphyria's Lover

Suggested content:

- Explore the cultural context of the poets, both writing in the 19th century (Browning male and Mew female). Both play on traditional 19th century concepts of women as homemakers and care givers. Porphyria is depicted as stereotypically beautiful by Victorian standards (blonde, blue eyed, long hair) and she brings fire, light and domesticity to the cottage. The farmer's wife is similarly described by her husband in terms of hair, eyes and the 'soft young down of her', but she does not conform to what is expected of her as a wife. After marriage she makes a break for freedom by running away.
- Further contrast in the way the poets depict female sexuality. In Browning's poem Porphyria makes herself sexually available and initiates sex. To do this outside of marriage would have shocked Victorian readers. In Mew's poem the speaker finds his wife extremely sexually attractive ('her eyes, her hair, her hair!') but she refuses to have marital sex – equally shocking for a Victorian audience. So both women adhere to, and rebel against, conforming to society, in completely different ways.
- Both poems are about oppression, control and capture of women. In their different ways, both male speakers are challenged by the difference and otherness of the females. In Browning's poem the speaker sees this in terms of power. Once he perceives that Porphyria worships him, he feels compelled to possess her (and therefore have power and control over her) for ever, by killing her. In the same way, the farmer in Mew's poem hunts down his fleeing wife, like a wild animal. He has the villagers to help him, so he knows society approves of his actions, and he makes no attempt to really understand her. She is then placed under lock and key and condemned to live in the marital home that she tried to escape. Both speakers display an arrogant, patriarchal right to control the freedom of the women they each eventually subdue.
- Porphyria and the farmer's bride come from very different backgrounds and inhabit utterly different parts of the social scale, yet they share significant characteristics in their portrayal as Victorian women.
- Poet's methods: Both Mew and Browning chose male speakers for their poems and chose to use the monologue form to present the narratives, so that in each poem the women are silent and the reader has to piece together and imagine the women's stories.

10. Sonnet 29/Letters from Yorkshire

Suggested content:

- Explore how both poets consider ways that long distance relationships can be maintained. Dooley is writing in the 20th century, but the 'he' of the poem corresponds by old-fashioned letters. Barrett Browning wrote sonnets to her then fiance Robert Browning, as a way of staying close to him. Both speakers address their 'him' directly as 'you', though Dooley begins her poem with the more distant pronouns 'he' and 'his' emphasising the physical distance between them. This lessens as the poem develops and it becomes clear that they are very close, so she uses the pronoun 'you' as a direct address.
- Compare the differences in the speakers' points of view: Barrett Browning presents a highly romantic view of a love relationship and her tone is excited and her language is flowery ('I think of thee!' and 'O my palm-tree'), whereas Dooley is at pains to stress the unromantic nature of her relationship with 'him' ('it's not romance, simply how things are') and her language is deliberately plain and pragmatic. There is a stillness and calmness to Dooley's speaker's tone compared to the effusiveness and longing of Barrett Browning's.
- Both speakers use thoughts to communicate with their partners and there is something metaphysical about the way that the couple in Dooley's poem 'tap out messages' with their souls, as if they have a shared understanding that is beyond words. Barrett Browning too sees thoughts as an important connector to her lover, but in her case the thoughts are likened to a vine that twists around his tree – a profoundly sexual image of possession and yearning to be close. This aspect of possession is absent in Dooley's poem, though the bond is no less strong. It is a different sort of relationship, based not on passion, but on being soul-mates.
- Both poets use natural imagery to convey the power of their feelings: Barrett Browning's vine bursts and shatters once her lover appears in person, because she no longer needs her thoughts to sustain her when he is actually in her presence. Dooley's speaker takes 'air and light' from his outdoor life in Yorkshire and with these 'pouring' from his letters. These are things that she doesn't have access to with her lifestyle. Barrett Browning's speaker too says that she breathes 'new air' when they are no longer separated.

11. Singh Song!/The Farmer's Bride

Suggested content:

- Explore how both poets use dramatic monologue to present their view of marriage: both are males talking about their wives. We do not hear the women's voices directly; all information is via their husbands.
- Both poets use dialect and non-standard English to create a characteristic voice of the speaker. In *Singh Song!* the speaker uses wordplay and puns and the tone is light-hearted. Her unconventionality, and the way she challenges cultural norms, is a source of joy and even pride in him. This compares to the speaker's attitude in *The Farmer's Bride*. Here the speaker uses details from the natural world, which is a world he understands, and his native dialect, to describe his wife, whose nature he does not understand. She does not behave as a conventional wife should and this is a source of unhappiness and confusion for him.
- The farmer says that he 'chose' his bride and there is no suggestion that it was a love match at the start, though he is sexually attracted to her. We sense that she was forced into the marriage by her eagerness to break free and the fact that she runs away. She was caught and returned home, but kept under lock and key and the marriage, as the farmer realises, is a sham. Compare with the marriage in *Singh Song!*: the newlyweds are very much in love and dream together of a different life – it is something they have in common, not something that drives them apart.
- Poet's methods: both use repetition, strong and regular rhythm, rhymes and internal rhymes and use a song or ballad form. This is particularly marked in *Singh Song!* with its use of refrain, that constantly reminds the speaker of his dull shop duties. The boisterous and exuberant tone of the poem reflects his wife's personality. With her Tartan sari and her red crew cut she is larger than life.
- The tone of *The Farmer's Bride* is more subdued, as the speaker is dimly aware that his wife is not happy but he is incapable of understanding her. He just wants a conventional, loving marriage and is confused about his wife's attitude.

12. Eden Rock/Before You Were Mine

Suggested content:

- Both poems are spoken by a child longing to be with parents. Both poets weave memories and imagined details from their childhood and use the present tense for impact and immediacy. Both are possibly inspired by a photograph of their parents.

- In Duffy's poem the daughter part imagines and part recalls, through her mother's memories, specific incidents from her mother's past before she gave birth to the daughter. Causley creates a tableau of his parents as young people and the dog on a family picnic, but he himself as a child is absent from the scene – he is on the other side of the bank, looking at them (just as the older poet does, but from across the years). Both speakers lovingly describe their parents through physical descriptions of their clothes, actions and words.
- Both poets vividly evoke a particular time when their parents were young and attractive, and full of life, and use specific details to illustrate the bond between them and their children. For Duffy the memory of playing with her mother's shoes and how her mother taught her dancing connects her to her mother's past. For Causley the link is expressed in almost spiritual tones, with the stream that separates them in the tableau taking on a symbolic status, as we realise his parents are dead and he, as an older man now, expects to join them on the other side eventually.
- Tone: Causley – the relationship is of him as a young child with his parents, and the memory is full of quiet, poignant recollection. Duffy – in contrast, rejoices in her mother's life 'before you were mine' and is almost envious of her mother's freedom then, wishing she could have been part of it. Hers is a possessive love: 'I wanted the bold girl winking in Portobello'.
- Poet's methods: Causley's language is quiet, contained and formal and his parents move slowly, 'leisurely' like an animated photograph. He refers to them rather stiffly as 'my mother' and 'my father'. Duffy's language sparkles and dances like her mother and she addresses her directly and informally, as a mother might address a daughter: 'whose small bites on your neck, sweetheart?'

13. Neutral Tones/Eden Rock

Suggested content:

- Similarities in setting – both natural, but Hardy's cold, wintry and colourless. Causley's imaginary and symbolic – *Eden Rock* references the Garden of Eden and its perfect innocence, as well as the Cornish moorland landscape of his birth. Hardy's setting is like a still life, inactive. The words spoken bring up bitter memories of the past: 'tedious riddles solved years ago'. Causley describes a photograph of a family picnic: his parents move slowly and call for him to join them across the stream.
- Similarities in mood: both speakers are sombre and quiet. Hardy's speaker sounds bitter and sad as he recalls how this love died long ago, and says this particular memory vividly continues to

remind him of the sadness of failed love. Causley's memory is an affectionate reminder of his parents when they were a young married couple and the details of H.P. Sauce bottle and thermos flask are tinged with nostalgia for another era.

- Contextual similarities and differences: Hardy's recalls an old love affair that continues to haunt him. Causley's parents are also dead and the poem has elegiac qualities of longing. The final line suggests a sense that he is looking forward to 'crossing' the stream to be with them again.
- Both use flashback to a very particular time and place and a vivid memory that encompasses a powerful set of reflective emotions. Use of significant detail to evoke a different era (tweed suit, straw hat, tin cups in Causley) and a specific day and place (sun, trees, leaves, pond and bird in Hardy).
- Structure and form – both poets use formal rhyme scheme. Hardy's is more tightly controlled with four verses, iambic pentameter suggesting a control of his feelings. Causley changes from four line verses to one longer verse, as the tone takes a mystical turn and final line is set apart with its devastating emotional impact.

14. Follower/Walking Away

Suggested content:

- Similarities: Both speakers recall a memory from the past. Heaney's childhood memory is of his father ploughing a field; Day Lewis's memory is of his son's football match when the speaker was a young parent. Heaney describes his father in detail – his power and expertise as a ploughman and the admiration he felt for him as a child. Day Lewis describes the emotional wrench he felt at the moment when he realised his son would become independent of his parents and explores the feelings he felt at the time.
- Show how both poets spend time in the past and the present to compare the emotions they felt then in the memory, and how those emotions have partly stayed and partly changed over time. Heaney shows this change by tense – past to present in the final verse, signalled by 'But today'. Day Lewis introduces the memory in the past ('It is eighteen years ago … since I watched you play'), but then uses the present tense to give immediacy to his description of his son's tentativeness and doubt as he took his first steps towards independence.
- Discuss how both poets express profound love, but in different ways. Heaney's speaker as a child admired his father's physical strength and dreamed of following in his footsteps; the speaker in *Walking Away* felt immense sympathy for his son's vulnerability.
- Both poems develop the thoughts and

emotions inspired by their memories to explore their ramifications through the years since. For Heaney, the roles have been reversed - his father now follows him, 'stumbling' in his wake and the implication is that his father is a nuisance (though a welcome one) just as the child was when he followed the plough. In *Walking Away*, the speaker admits that he has struggled to decode what he found so troubling about that particular parting. He concludes that the hardest part of love is the 'letting go', just as was 'proved' (in his belief) by God's sacrifice of his Son to save mankind.

- Structure: Heaney's poem is a tribute to his father's expertise in more ways than one, since it shows his mastery of form and technique: a regular rhyme pattern and four-line verses with use of alliteration and assonance to create the rhythmical jingling sound of the plough. Day Lewis's poem is also formal with rhythmical pattern and a regular rhyme scheme reflecting that he has controlled and made sense of those feelings that overcame him in the past.

15. Before You Were Mine/Mother, any distance

Suggested content:

- Say that the two poems are written by speakers about their mothers. Armitage's speaker is grown up and moving into his first home. He is testing his feelings about independence and separation from his mother. Duffy is also adult. She draws on childhood memories of her mother to imagine that time in her mother's life before the speaker was born. Both poets explore the complexities of their feelings for their mothers and in the process their mothers' love for them.
- Explore how the poets use metaphor and imagery to suggest the strength of the bond between parent and child. Duffy's mother is full of life and energy and the speaker imagines her very glamorous and sparkling life of boyfriends in the late 1940s dances, and staying out late. This was all before her mother's life changed. It was 'The decade ahead of my loud, possessive yell' when she gave birth to the speaker. There is no sense in the poem that the mother resented this change in her life. Duffy recalls how her mother would teach her dance steps and let her play with her shoes. Still, the speaker oddly yearns for the mother she never knew: 'the bold girl winking in Portobello'. It is as if Duffy is trying to understand what that change might have meant to her mother and it makes her realise how much her mother must have loved her.
- Armitage: The poet uses an extended metaphor of a measuring tape to suggest the tenuous, stretched

connection between mother and son. It is very effective because in a way the tape measures the ' years between us', emphasising their shared history. The speaker starts out by acknowledging that he's not quite ready yet to leave that 'second pair of hands' that he needs now to measure his new house. As he moves up the storeys, the line becomes tighter and he imagines his mother holding on to her end – and her connection with him – to breaking point. This powerfully illustrates the strength of her love for him and his confidence in her that she will try to keep hold of him, and in contact with him, for as long as she can.

- Structure and form: Armitage's poem starts out as a sonnet, a form traditionally used to express romantic love. This is significant as he uses it to express the love he feels for his mother. His mother has been a constant support for him and he acknowledges this further by the image he uses for each of them – she is his anchor, he her kite. He imaginatively uses the sonnet form to offer a personal view on love between parent and child, deliberately disrupting the form as the poem develops, to mirror how the speaker gradually moves towards independence.
- Duffy: regular line length of verses, but no discernible rhyme scheme or rhythmic pattern, allowing a conversational, informal and intimate structure that reflects the closeness of the mother-daughter relationship.

Glossary

A

Alliteration   repetition of a sound at the beginning of words

Analysis   a close examination of the meaning, style, form and effects of a poem

Annotate   to add critical or explanatory notes to a poem

Antithesis   a contrast of ideas

Assonance   repetition of vowel sounds

C

Caesura   a pause in a line of poetry – usually in the middle of a line, but sometimes at the start

Comparison   when two or more different things are compared for their similarities

Consonance   repetition of consonants

Contrast   when two or more different things are compared for their differences

Conversational   as used in a conversation; informal

Cultural   relating to the traditions and beliefs of a society

D

Dramatic monologue   a poem where two voices are heard, often revealing aspects of their characters and details of events leading up to the current situation

E

End-stopped   the end of a sentence or clause which coincides with the end of a line in a poem

Enjambment   when a clause or sentence runs from one line of poetry to another, undisturbed by punctuation

Extended metaphor   a comparison between two unlike things that is sustained over an entire poem

F

First person   a narrative viewpoint where the narrator is involved and refers to 'I' or 'me'

Form   the physical structure of a poem composed of line length, rhyme, rhythm and repetition

I

Idiolect   features of speech unique to an individual

Imagery   a collection of devices (including metaphor, simile, personification, synecdoche and onomatopoeia) which use language to create vivid visual descriptions

Imperative (verb)   a verb used to give orders, commands or instructions

Irregular rhyme   rhyming that follows a fixed pattern

J

Juxtaposition   the placement of words or ideas close together for comparison or contrast

L

Lyric poem   expresses heightened personal emotions or thoughts of the speaker

M

Metaphor   a form of imagery where one thing is said to be another, suggesting similarities between the two

Metre   the arrangement of syllables in a line of poetry according to a number of beats

Monologue   spoken by one person

Monosyllable   one syllable

Mood   the feeling created in a poem through word choice and theme

N

Non-standard English   English that breaks the rules of the standard form accepted as correct by educated users

O

Oxymoron   the use of words which have contrasting meanings in order to emphasise one meaning, e.g. 'a deafening silence'

P

Pathetic fallacy   attributing feelings to non-human things, especially the weather (from 'pathos' – 'to feel')

Perception   a belief, or opinion, often held by many people and based on how things seem or appear

Persona   a character (not the poet) who is the speaker of a poem

Personification   a form of imagery that gives animals, ideas or inanimate objects human qualities

Possessive pronoun   a word that shows ownership

Prepositions   show the relationship in direction, location or time between a noun and other words in a sentence

Present tense   a verb tense that says what is happening now

Presentation   the style used by the poet to present a poem

Pronoun   a word that takes the place of a noun

Q

Quatrain   a group of four lines

R

Repetition   the simple repeating of a word within a line, verse or entire poem

Rhetorical question   a question asked for effect or emphasis with no answer expected

Rhyme   correspondence of sounds between words or word endings

Rhythm   a pattern of stressed and unstressed syllables that creates a beat

S

Sestet   a group of six lines of poetry

Sibilance   a type of alliteration that uses 's' sounds ('s', 'sh', soft 'ch' and soft 'c') to create a hissing sound

Simile   a direct comparison of one thing to another, using the words 'as', 'like', or 'than'

Sonnet   a poem of fourteen lines arranged in one of certain definite rhyme schemes, e.g. octet followed by sestet; three quatrains followed by a couplet, etc.

Stressed syllable   a syllable in a word that is pronounced with greater force than other syllables

T

Third person   a narrative viewpoint where the narrator is uninvolved and people are referred to as 'he', 'she', 'they', etc.

V

Voice   the style and tone (through word choice, rhyme and stylistic features) by which a poet creates the character of a speaker

Index

A
Alliteration 22-23, 40-41, 54-55
Analysis 72-75
Antithesis 22-23
Assonance 24-25, 40-41

B
Before You Were Mine 44-45

C
Caesura 24-25
Climbing My Grandfather 59-61
Comparing poems 72-75
Comparison grids 73
Consonance 54-55
Contrast 28-29, 44-45

D
Dramatic monologue 6, 12-14, 56-58

E
Eden Rock 38-39
Enjambment 12-14, 15-17, 24-25, 28-29
Extended metaphor 15-17, 42-43, 59-61

F
First person 15-17
Follower 40-41
Form 6

I
Idiolect 56-58
Imagery 42-43, 44-45
Imperatives 10-11

J
Juxtaposition 38-39

L
Letters from Yorkshire 28-29
Love's Philosophy 10-11
Lyric poem 22-23

M
Metaphor 56-58
Metre 38-39
Monologue 24-25
Monosyllables 8-9, 10-11
Mood 6
Mother, any distance 42-43

N
Neutral Tones 22-23

O
Older poetry 5
Oxymoron 22-23

P
Pathetic fallacy 10-11
Personification 10-11
Planning answers 74
Porphyria's Lover 12-14
Possessive pronoun 56-58
Prepositions 59-61
Present tense 38-39, 44-45
Pronouns 28-29

Q
Quatrain 15-17

R
Repetition 10-11, 15-17, 26-27, 8-9
Rhetorical questions 10-11
Rhyme 8-9, 12-14, 40-41
Rhythm 12-14, 40-41

S
Sestet 15-17
Sibilance 24-25
Simile 24-25, 26-27, 54-55, 59-61
Singh Song! 56-58
Sonnet 6, 15-17, 42-43
Sonnet 29 – 'I think of Thee!' 15-17
Stressed syllables 8-9

T
Technique 6
The Farmer's Bride 24-25
Themes 6-7
Third person 28-29
Tone 72

V
Voice 6, 24-25

W
Walking Away 26-27
When We Two Parted 8-9
Winter Swans 54-55
Writing answers 75